THE MANCHESTER RAILWAY

THE CALDER VALLEY LINE

Martin Bairstow

2-6-4T No 42285 is signalled towards Greetland as it passes Dryclough Junction on 8 August 1964 with through carriages from Halifax to Kings Cross
(Martin Bairstow Collection)

Published by Martin Bairstow, 53 Kirklees Drive, Farsley, Leeds
Printed by The Amadeus Press, Cleckheaton, West Yorkshire

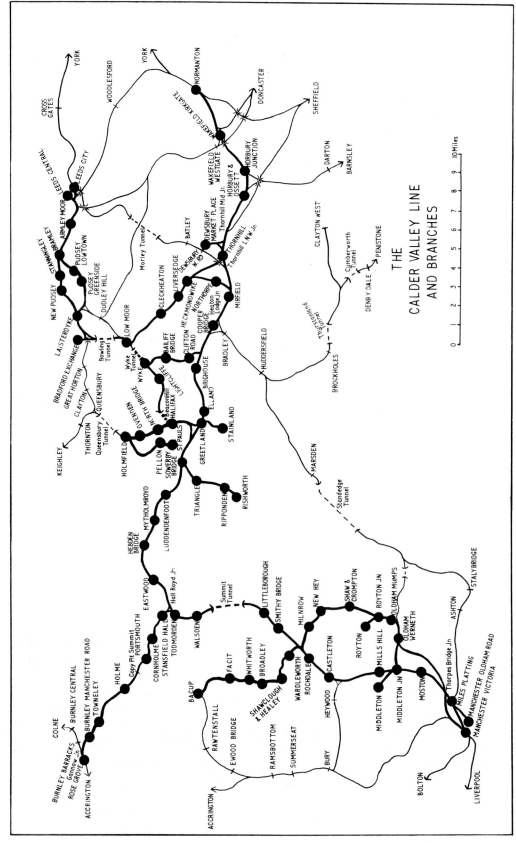

THE
CALDER VALLEY LINE
AND BRANCHES

The Castleton to Heywood and Miles Platting to Stalybridge lines were both built by the Manchester & Leeds Railway, opening in 1842 and 1846 respectively. They are not featured in the present book because their subsequent histories linked them more appropriately to other titles in the series.

2

Introduction

The Manchester & Leeds was the first Trans Pennine Railway. At its opening in 1841, Summit Tunnel was the longest in the World. The line had been built under the guidance of George Stephenson who preferred minimum gradients at the expense of a circuitous route (60 miles) missing some of the towns en route such as Oldham and Halifax.

The line followed the Calder Valley from Walsden all the way to Wakefield. Access to Leeds was by running powers from Goose Hill Junction, Normanton because authority to build the final 10½ miles had been granted to the North Midland Railway.

The Manchester & Leeds changed its name to the Lancashire & Yorkshire Railway in 1847 to reflect its broadening sphere of operation. In that guise it remained an independent company until amalgamation with the London & North Western Railway in 1922.

It gained a shorter route into Leeds in 1848 but only by running powers over the Leeds & Dewsbury. It lost the opportunity to purchase that line preferring to press on with its own route to Leeds via Halifax and Bradford. This was achieved in 1854 but, again, only by running powers from Bowling Junction over what became a part of the Great Northern Railway.

This book treats as the main line the route from Manchester Victoria both to Leeds via Halifax and through the lower Calder Valley to Normanton. Branch lines are dealt with in separate chapters. The book is both revised and enlarged from the edition which appeared in 1987.

Farsley, Leeds

Martin Bairstow
February 2001

Contents

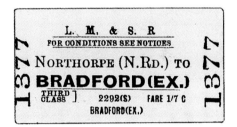

L. M. & S. R
FOR CONDITIONS SEE NOTICES
1377
NORTHORPE (N. Rd.) TO
BRADFORD (EX.)
THIRD CLASS]   2292(S)   FARE 1/7 C
BRADFORD (EX.)
1377

0-6-0 No. 715, built by Kitson & Co of Leeds in 1871, at the head of a Burnley train at the east end of Todmorden Station about 1890. For a time, the engine carried the name 'Medusa' whilst working on the East Lancashire section of the L&Y.

(B.C. Lane collection)

Refranchising

This revised edition is being written during the closing months of 2000. At a time of rapid change, some details could be out of date before they are even printed.

Passenger trains were franchised in March 1997 when Regional Railways North East passed from BR ownership to MTL Trust Holdings Ltd. The name Northern Spirit was introduced in 1998. By the end of 1999, MTL was in financial difficulties and in February 2000 Northern Spirit became part of the Arriva Group supposedly for 12 months only pending refranchising.

Meanwhile Regional Railways North West had gone to Great Western Holdings which was partly owned by First Group. When the latter bought out its co owners, the name was changed to First North Western.

At the moment, Northern Spirit and First North Western share the local services, more or less on a geographical basis but Northern Spirit has the 'Trans Pennine Express' routes.

Under refranchising, 'Trans Pennine Express' is to become a separate business whilst the Northern Spirit and First North Western local functions are to merge. It is not clear into which franchise the Leeds–Blackpool service will fall.

The freight operation was sold in 1996 to English, Welsh & Scottish Railway which is substantially owned by Wisconsin Central. There are suggestions that this organisation will change hands.

In a different age, the Manchester & Leeds Railway was incorporated in 1836. It changed its name in 1847 but otherwise retained its independent identity until the last day of 1921. It was then part of the London & North Western Railway for one year, the London Midland & Scottish Railway for 25 years and British Railways for nearly half a century until the privatisation process began.

Great Northern suburban electric No. 313052 can work off both overhead wires and third rail. It requires a class 40 to haul it westbound through Brighouse in 1981. Nowadays, movements like this, to and from Works can be so complicated that rolling stock is sometimes conveyed by road. *(Martin Bairstow)*

Two 'black fives' wait to draw their empty stock out of Cheetham Hill carriage sidings. The Manchester loop line is to the left of the carriage shed. Sister engine 45108 is emerging from Queens Road Carriage Sidings. *(R.S. Greenwood)*

The frontage of Manchester Victoria completed in 1909. The lower level building on the extreme left is part of the original 1844 station.
(Martin Bairstow)

A class 104 unit leaving platform 7 in the suburban part of Victoria Station, 1983.
(Martin Bairstow)

Viewed from platform 11, across the through lines leading to Exchange Station, D311 stands at platform 12 with a Blackpool train on 24 February 1963.
(Martin Bairstow collection)

A Journey from Manchester Victoria to Leeds

In the Year 2000

Few passengers make the full journey of 1 hour 30 minutes for 49½ miles with 12 stops. Most of those for Leeds and beyond will prefer the 'Trans Pennine Express' from Manchester Piccadilly which is both faster and more frequent. Whether there should be an express by the Calder Valley route is a question which will come up later in the book.

For the present, we must make do with a stopping service catering for intermediate traffic, much of it short distance but including journeys such as Manchester to Bradford and Rochdale to Leeds which deserve better. If we travel in an evening or on Sunday, there are no local trains between Manchester and Rochdale so our service becomes all stations – 1 hour 35 minutes with 15 stops.

The train is often a class 155 two coach diesel multiple unit of which seven examples were supplied by Leyland in 1988 for the West Yorkshire PTE, in whose red livery they appear. When they wanted to order ten more, Leyland declined so instead the PTE got ten air conditioned 158s identical to those on the 'Trans Pennine' routes except that they have bicycle space instead of the second toilet. These also appear in PTE livery and turn up on the Calder Valley route. By far the smartest examples of rolling stock currently seen regularly are the recently refurbished class 156 units. Built in the late 1980s, these now have bright interiors and carry a blue Northern Spirit livery.

Manchester Victoria has changed considerably since the previous edition of this book, published in 1987. Express and long distance trains were transferred around 1990 to Piccadilly Station. The remaining local services have increased in frequency. The biggest change is the replacement of the Bury electrics by the Metrolink light rail system. This arrives from Bury on more or less the site of the old platforms 5 and 6. Then it takes a sharp right angle curve to exit the station through a hole in the side wall. It traverses the City Centre as a street tramway running every 12 minutes (15 minutes on Sundays) to Piccadilly Station. Except evenings and Sundays, there is also a 12 minute interval service from Bury direct to Altrincham, also serving Victoria so giving a 6 minute interval through the City Centre. The trams have a distinctive whistle which sounds a bit like a Gresley Pacific when running in street mode. They use a more conventional horn when running on the 'normal' railway line to Bury.

The main concourse and suburban part of Victoria still look as though they've not been repaired after Second World War bomb damage. Platforms 1 to 8 have been swept away leaving only 9 and 10 (now numbered 1 and 2) in use by some trains to Oldham, Stalybridge, Rochdale and the Calder Valley. A substantial part of the original 1844 station building remains in use.

Metrolink has an island platform labelled B and C but B is little used. Trams arriving from Piccadilly use platform A which is at right angles adjoining the concourse.

The main line station, comprising the old platforms 11 to 17, has been rebuilt completely. There are four through platforms, now numbered 3 to 6, above which has been built the Arena entertainment centre. There are passenger operated lifts to assist people who need to use the footbridge to reach the further platforms. It is intended that, eventually, the remainder of the

station will be brought up to the same standard.

At the eastern exit from Victoria, there is no longer a choice of route. Most Calder Valley trains used to take the 'loop line' direct to Thorpes Bridge Junction but this was closed in 1998. The wide trackless formation is still visible. Further north it will come back into use when the Oldham branch is connected to Metrolink.

Our train attacks the 1 in 47 Miles Platting bank which required rope haulage when first opened in 1844. At Collyhurst Junction, the original Manchester & Leeds Railway joins on the right. Closed to passengers in 1844, it survived for goods until 1982. The first few yards of the branch were relaid as part of the Manchester area remodelling in 1998. The new, unused tracks seem just to disappear into the undergrowth. In fact they actually serve as a headshunt for a Tilcon Stone terminal which is not at present used.

The Stalybridge line goes off at Miles Platting. This carries a local passenger service, half hourly to Stalybridge, hourly to Huddersfield and Wakefield. A triangular junction is completed by the sharp double track curve which comes in at Brewery Junction (formerly Brewery Sidings).

The 1998 resignalling swept away the portakabin type signal box at Thorpes Bridge Junction where the Oldham branch diverges. Newton Heath motive power depot is in the angle formed by the Leeds and Oldham lines. Moston Station is in a sorry state, dilapidated and unstaffed.

Vitriol Works is now the fringe signal box to the Manchester power signalled area. It is named after the one time works of Hannibal Becker & Co. There is little visible trace of Middleton Junction which had branches diverging at both sides. The station had curving branch platforms to the Oldham line which included the 1 in 27 Werneth incline. Trains to Middleton itself used the main line platforms at Middleton Junction then diverged to the left immediately north of the station.

In the earliest days of the M&L Railway, before the branches were built to either Oldham or Middleton, there was a short lived station at Mills Hill, the nearest point on the main line to both. In 1985 a new station was built at the same point, 143 years after previously booking its last passenger.

Before Castleton there is a triangular junction with the Heywood branch. A large permanent way and rail welding depot is located alongside the North Junction to East Junction curve. The triangular layout is retained because continuous welded rail sometimes has to be despatched with the wagons facing a particular direction. Beyond Castleton North Junction the branch towards Heywood is disused apart from stock movements to and from the preserved East Lancashire Railway.

Rochdale Station was rebuilt in 1980 but reduced in size with all traffic concentrated on one of the previous two island platforms. A bay is retained at the east end for trains starting out onto the Oldham branch. This diverges at Rochdale signal box, the former Rochdale Goods Yard Box.

Little trace remains on the opposite side of the start of the line to Bacup which passed, near Britannia Station, over the highest summit on the Lancashire & Yorkshire Railway – 965 feet above sea level.

Since leaving Manchester the line has been on an ascending gradient. It was steepest between Victoria Station and Miles Platting with a maximum of 1 in 47 but there have been several miles at around 1 in 150.

A Manchester to Oldham dmu near the top of Miles Platting 'bank' on 7 June 1984. The original Manchester & Leeds route from Oldham Road terminus joined the line from Victoria at Collyhurst Junction.
(G.W. Morrison)

Miles Platting Station viewed from the Stalybridge line platforms in August 1968.
(G.C. Lewthwaite)

A 1961 view of Newton Heath motive power depot. By that time 12 of the original 24 roads had been removed to make way for the dmu servicing depot.
(Ian G. Holt)

Beyond Rochdale there is a two mile level stretch which used to include the water troughs at Clegg Hall. The level stretch continues through Smithy Bridge station which reopened in 1985 after closure in 1961. A modest climb at 1 in 330 prevails for 4½ miles through Littleborough and on to the highest point on the route which is reached at the Yorkshire portal of the 2,885 yard Summit Tunnel. Only a few yards beyond the main tunnel is the 41 yard Summit East closely followed by Dean Royd Tunnel which is 70 yards in length. The line now emerges into a very narrow twisting valley. Winterbutlee Tunnel leads to the village of Walsden where the station reopened in 1990 after an absence of 29 years. Gauxholme Viaduct has 18 arches, the first spanning the Rochdale Canal. This waterway is almost immediately recrossed by a turreted bridge with its original cast iron girders, still in situ but relieved of any load.

Todmorden used to have a loop and a bay platform on the up (Manchester) side from which trains started to Burnley and East Lancashire until withdrawal in 1965. The ticket office is now on the Manchester bound platform, a bit inconvenient for Leeds direction passengers who have to negotiate two lots of stairs. Previously it was at ground level near the entrance. Look across to the Queens Hotel on the right and you can just make out the blocked up opening on the upper floor which once had direct access by a foot bridge from the station platform.

There is a nine arch viaduct between Todmorden Station and the former junction with the Burnley, or Copy Pit, line. The direct curve from Todmorden East is lifted but the other line still curves in at Hall Royd Junction. Preston power box controls the Copy Pit route together with a section of the Manchester to Leeds line bounded by Smithy Bridge and Hebden Bridge boxes.

The Calder Valley is so narrow that there is barely room for the railway as well as the river, the Rochdale Canal and the road. There are three tunnels before the site of Eastwood Station which had very low platforms. At Charlestown the line passes round a hillside through which it was impossible to tunnel. It reverts to tunnelling when it encounters a similar obstacle at Weasel Hall. The train then arrives at Hebden Bridge where the station, with partially staggered platforms, is painted in an attractive white and black – not the standard house style. The valley becomes a little wider but still the railway, river, canal and road stick close together through Mytholmroyd.

The station here was moved in 1990, a short distance towards Halifax to give easier access avoiding the winding staircase in the old building which still stands.

On the approach to Sowerby Bridge Tunnel, the Wainhouse Tower, a folly with no utilitarian purpose, appears on the hillside to the left. Also visible to the left of this is St Paul's Church which lent its name to the terminus of the Halifax High Level Railway.

Emerging from the Tunnel, Sowerby Bridge engine shed stood on the left whilst the goods yard was on the right hand side of the main line. Here also was

40002 backing out of Cheetham Hill carriage sidings with the stock of the 10.20 Manchester Victoria to Newcastle on 4 September 1982. The Manchester 'loop line' is on the right.

(G.W. Morrison)

The 10.30 Liverpool Exchange to Newcastle express passing Newton Heath hauled by 'Patriot' class 4-6-0 No. 45517 on 10 August 1958.

(Peter Hutchinson)

1930s architecture pervades at Moston Station through which a class 40 is passing with tankers for Stanlow in June 1981. The station has deteriorated considerably since.

(R.S.Greenwood)

the site of the pre 1876 passenger station.

The replacement station was designed to be junction between two main lines. But the plan to build the Rishworth branch through to Rochdale was abandoned at an early stage. The station buildings, located in the angle between the main line and the Rishworth branch had become an eyesore prior to demolition about 1981. A new booking office was provided but the station became unstaffed in 1985. The bricked up tunnel on the Rishworth branch can be glimpsed from the station which has been tidied up and provided with a new car park.

One mile from Sowerby Bridge, the Leeds train leaves the Calder Valley at Milner Royd Junction and a gradient of 1 in 120 takes it across Copley Viaduct and through the site of Copley station, closed in 1931. The line to Wakefield can be seen in the valley below until our train enters Bank House Tunnel through which it curves sharply to the left.

Emerging back in to the open, the steep branch from Greetland is below on our right. It joins at Dryclough Junction. We approach Halifax through a deep rock cutting. On the left the original Shaw Syke terminus is derelict but the goods yard has become the site for the Eureka Childrens Museum which, since 1994, has provided Halifax Station with some additional custom.

The main station building at Halifax dates from 1855. It was partly obscured from view in the 1880s when the station was enlarged and a new forecourt built on a viaduct over the goods lines. Since the late 1960s, all railway business has been conducted from the further island platform leaving the main building derelict. During 2000 this has been refurbished for use as offices. As well as removing an eyesore, these should generate additional passenger traffic.

Leaving the one surviving island platform the line

curves to the right over the ten arch Bailcliff Viaduct. To the left is the stub of the long viaduct which carried the L & Y and GN joint line to Holmfield. Straight ahead is the turreted entrance to Beacon Hill Tunnel. Crossing the Shibden Valley on an embankment, the railway takes a long sweep to the right towards Hipperholme where the only surviving relic of the former station is the house on the left hand side, once occupied by the station master.

Hipperholme Tunnel is followed by a curve to the left. Another short tunnel leads through the site of Lightcliffe Station. A long straight stretch takes the line over the Hall Bottom Viaduct, from which we can see part of the substantial Wyke Viaduct on the ill fated Brighouse to Pickle Bridge branch. The greater part of the structure was demolished in the late 1980s having stood disused for nearly 40 years.

The station master's house at Wyke & Norwood Green is still in use as a private residence. The downstairs windows are at track level. Emerging from the 1,365 yard Wyke Tunnel, there is a short Furnace Tunnel before the train comes upon the complex which was Low Moor.

The engine shed was on the left of the station which had two island platforms. Six signal boxes controlled the layout which included a triangular junction with the Spen Valley branch. To the right of the former station stands the ill fated 'Transperience' museum. Opened in 1995 it only lasted two years. Visitor numbers were grossly over estimated. It was a lesson in how to waste public money. Beyond is the former Great Northern goods warehouse, now occupied as a factory. The Great Northern branch to Dudley Hill was closed to all traffic as early as 1917. Its alignment was more or less that now used by the road out of the Transperience car park.

During 1952 Chadderton Power Station Sidings were extended and a replacement signal box was commissioned at Vitriol Works. Stanier 2-6-4T No. 42629 passes on a Middleton to Manchester local comprising L&Y, LMS and LNW coaches.
(J. Davenport)

Aspinall 2-4-2 radial tank No. 1271 has just left Moston with a local for Bury via Heywood in June 1915. The train comprises three 'Oldham bogies' with narrow bodies for the restricted clearances which beset the Oldham line at that time.
(B.C. Lane collection)

Chadderton No. 1, a Barclay 0-4-0ST in the power station sidings in 1952. *(J. Davenport)*

Aspinall 4-4-0 No. 1096 (built 1891) approaching Middleton Junction with a York to Manchester express about 1918. *(B.C. Lane collection)*

Middleton Junction West box stood in the angle of the junction with the Oldham line. It was built in 1882, remaining in use until 1987. Road traffic still has to negotiate the narrow under bridge. *(B C Lane collection)*

8F 2-8-0 No. 48530 passing Castleton in May 1961 with a Saturday afternoon freight from Bolton to Healey Mills. The loco had recently passed through Horwich Works.
(Ian G. Holt)

Standard 2-6-0 No. 78043 pulling into Castleton on the 15.45 Rochdale to Wigan Wallgate via Bury on 3 April 1961. *(Ian G. Holt)*

The distance from Halifax to Bradford is 8 miles, of which 2½ are in tunnels. The longest of these, at 1,648 yards is Bowling, from which the line emerges to make the descent at 1 in 50 to Bradford. Prior to dieselisation, Leeds trains left the Lancashire & Yorkshire Railway at Bowling Junction, avoiding the climb in and out of Bradford which was served by separate portions. Bradford and Leeds trains were divided either at Halifax or Low Moor.

Bradford Exchange has been known as Interchange since 1983 because it is part of a bus/rail complex. The bus station which stands on the site of the L&Y Bridge Street goods depot, has been reduced in size during recent rebuilding. The previous railway terminus, in use prior to 1973, was situated beyond the present buffer stops and was characterised by its double arched overall roof.

After reversal at Bradford, the train retraces its steps a short way to Mill Lane Junction then takes the sharp curve through St Dunstans where there was a station with separate branch platforms on the GNR Queensbury line. This passed underneath the L&Y descending from Bowling Junction and made a triangle by rejoining the Bradford to Leeds line a little further on in a cutting. Wakefield Road Tunnel brings the tracks past the site of Hammerton Street engine shed which is now a bus depot.

The alignment from the original Leeds, Bradford & Halifax Junction terminus at Bradford Adolphus Street is joined for the 1 in 44 climb to Laisterdyke. Here there was a station with two island platforms situated in the cutting at the summit of the line. The station master's house can be seen at road level up on the right.

Once past Laisterdyke the train changes gear and picks up speed down the 1 in 100 towards Hillfoot

Tunnel but the brakes are soon applied for the stop at New Pudsey. A viaduct leads onto the site of Stanningley Station, now completely abandoned. The next station, Bramley, fared better being one of the wooden unstaffed halts reinstated under a programme sponsored by the West Yorkshire PTE. Beyond the site of Armley Moor Station the gradient increases to 1 to 50. The curve between Wortley West and South Junctions, giving direct running from Bradford Interchange to London is abandoned. Copley Hill engine shed was located in the angle formed by the electrified route from Doncaster which we join at Holbeck West Junction.

Prior to 1967, our line ran into Leeds Central crossing over the Midland Skipton to Leeds City route at Holbeck where there was a two level interchange station. This closed in 1958. When Leeds Central closed in 1967, the tracks were diverted to descend and join the Midland at Whitehall Junction and so gain access to Leeds City which became the sole passenger station in Leeds.

The scheme to combine the two Leeds stations was done on the cheap. Under the original 1959 plan, the line from Bradford would have used a flyover rather than cross the Midland on the level. The job was halted then reappraised during the Beeching period when it was assumed that many passenger trains would disappear. The result was a severely congested layout which has been an increasing problem for over 30 years. Eventually, in 1999 Railtrack embarked on a major plan to increase capacity with six tracks instead of four at the western approach with the number of platforms increased from 12 to 17. Also involved are a new roof and improved passenger facilities including lifts and escalators. The project is schedule for completion at the end of 2001.

'Crab' 2-6-0 No. 42706 stands at Rochdale with the 8.45pm Manchester Victoria to Bradford and Leeds on 31 December 1961, the last day of steam on this service. *(R.S. Greenwood)*

English Electric Type 3 (now class 37) No. D6864 passing a Liverpool Exchange to Harrogate dmu in Rochdale Station on 19 August 1967. All trains now use the left hand of the two island platforms. *(Ian G. Holt)*

Midland 3F 0-6-0 No. 43734 stands in the bay platform at the east end of Rochdale Station with a parcels train for Stoke on 17 July 1961. The Cravens dmu is on the Manchester via Oldham service. *(Ian G. Holt)*

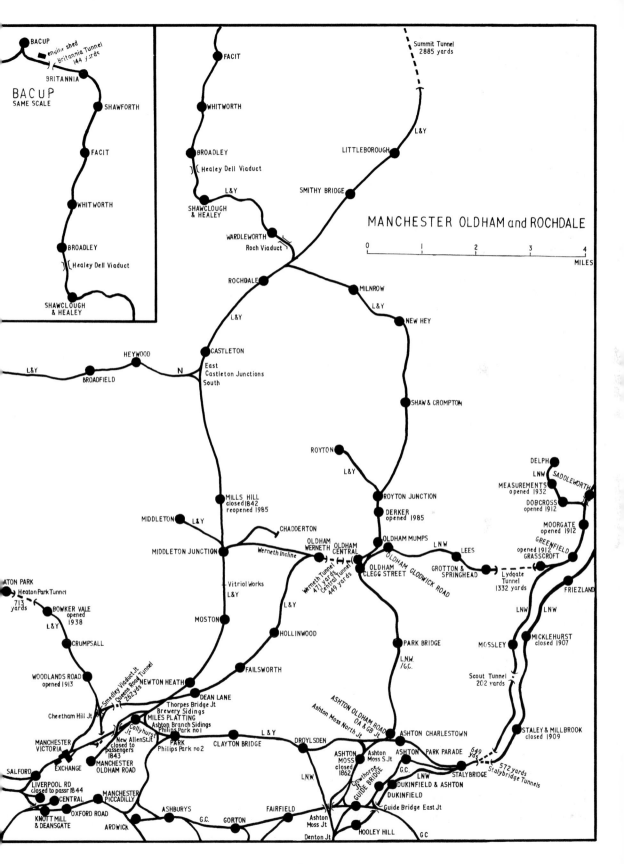

BACUP
SAME SCALE

BACUP
engine shed
Britannia Tunnel 144 yards
BRITANNIA
SHAWFORTH
FACIT
WHITWORTH
BROADLEY
(Healey Dell Viaduct
SHAWCLOUGH & HEALEY

FACIT
WHITWORTH
BROADLEY
)(Healey Dell Viaduct
SHAWCLOUGH & HEALEY
L&Y
WARDLEWORTH
Roch Viaduct
ROCHDALE
L&Y
CASTLETON
East Castleton Junctions South
N
HEYWOOD
BROADFIELD
L&Y

Summit Tunnel 2885 yards
L&Y
LITTLEBOROUGH
SMITHY BRIDGE

MANCHESTER OLDHAM and ROCHDALE

0   1   2   3   4
MILES

MILNROW
L&Y
NEW HEY

SHAW & CROMPTON

ROYTON
L&Y
ROYTON JUNCTION
DERKER opened 1985
OLDHAM MUMPS
LNW
LEES
GROTTON & SPRINGHEAD
Lyddate Tunnel 1332 yards

DELPH
LNW
SADDLEWORTH
MEASUREMENTS opened 1932
DOBCROSS opened 1912
MOORGATE opened 1912
GREENFIELD opened 1912
GRASSCROFT
FRIEZLAND

MILLS HILL closed 1842 reopened 1985
MIDDLETON
L&Y
CHADDERTON
MIDDLETON JUNCTION
Werneth Incline
OLDHAM WERNETH
OLDHAM CENTRAL
Werneth Tunnel 471 yards
Central Tunnel 449 yards
OLDHAM CLEGG STREET
OLDHAM GLODWICK ROAD

Vitriol Works
L&Y

ATON PARK
Heaton Park Tunnel 713 yards
BOWKER VALE opened 1938
L&Y
CRUMPSALL
WOODLANDS ROAD opened 1913

MOSTON
HOLLINWOOD
L&Y
FAILSWORTH

PARK BRIDGE
LNW /GC.
MOSSLEY
Scout Tunnel 202 yards

MICKLEHURST closed 1907
LNW
LNW
STALEY & MILLBROOK closed 1909

Smedley Viaduct Jt
Queens Road Tunnel 262 yds
NEWTON HEATH
DEAN LANE
Thorpes Bridge Jt
Brewery Sidings
MILES PLATTING
Cheetham Hill Jt
New Allen St Jt
Collyhurst
Ashton Branch Sidings
Philips Park no1

MANCHESTER VICTORIA
closed to passengers 1843
EXCHANGE
SALFORD
LIVERPOOL RD closed to passr 1844
CENTRAL
OXFORD ROAD
KNOTT MILL & DEANSGATE
MANCHESTER OLDHAM ROAD
PARK
Philips Park no2
MANCHESTER PICCADILLY
ASHBURYS
ARDWICK
GORTON
G.C.

CLAYTON BRIDGE
L&Y
DROYLSDEN
FAIRFIELD
LNW
Ashton Moss Jt
Denton Jt

ASHTON OLDHAM ROAD
OA & GB Jt
Ashton Moss North Jt
ASHTON CHARLESTOWN
ASHTON MOSS closed 1862
Ashton Moss S Jt
Crowthorne
GUIDE BRIDGE
ASHTON PARK PARADE
DUKINFIELD & ASHTON
Guide Bridge East Jt
DUKINFIELD
HOOLEY HILL
649 yds
STALYBRIDGE
572 yards Stalybridge Tunnels
G.C.
LNW
G C

Smithy Bridge looking towards Todmorden in 1959. Since rebuilding in 1985 the Leeds bound platform has been on the near side of the level crossing. *(G.W. Morrison)*

Two black fives on the 14.02 York to Liverpool Exchange. 44823 and 45103 passing Summit West on 25 March 1961. *(Ian G. Holt)*

Summit Tunnel

The optimistic forecasts of the engineers who built the railway through Summit (page 14) were put to the test on the early morning of 20 December 1984 when a tanker train became derailed inside the tunnel. The train crew escaped then went back into the tunnel and rescued the engine and some of the wagons not knowing the risk they were taking. Shortly afterwards the remaining wagons were on fire and continued to burn for almost a week. The whole tunnel became a furnace and flames leapt through the ventilation shafts.

Traffic was suspended between Rochdale and Todmorden but when an emergency timetable was eventually produced from 21 January, trains were restored to Littleborough. Fears that the tunnel was damaged beyond repair proved ill founded thanks to the thickness of the brick lining. Through traffic was restored on 19 August 1985 when Smithy Bridge Station also reopened.

WD 2-8-0 No. 90181 emerges from the west portal of Summit Tunnel on 13 December 1963.
(Ian G. Holt)

A WD 2-8-0 crossing Gauxholme Viaduct, south of Todmorden, with a coal train. The skew arch dates from the opening of the line but was strengthened in 1905 by the addition of girders below rail level. *(R.S. Greenwood)*

WD 2-8-0 No. 90726 passing Todmorden eastbound with coal empties, early 1960s. A Cravens dmu has worked in from the Copy Pit line.   *(R.S. Greenwood)*

8F 2-8-0 No. 48139 heads a Mirfield to Garston freight past Hall Royd Junction on 13 October 1962.
(R.S. Greenwood)

Mytholmroyd Station looking towards Halifax. Passengers reach the platform by a winding staircase inside the main building. *(G.C. Lewthwaite)*

A WD 2-8-0 passing Luddendenfoot in 1951. *(Station UK)*

The 1876 station building at Sowerby Bridge, photographed in April 1979. Not long after, it was demolished, just as the Government was about to put a listed building preservation order on it. *(Alan Young)*

Through the Lower Calder Valley

'Black Five' 4-6-0 No. 45101 heading coal empties along the Main line between Milner Royd and Greetland on 9 January 1964. Copley Viaduct and the Wainhouse tower are to the right.
(Martin Bairstow collection)

There is no present day equivalent to the 'Through Dining Car Express', which used to connect Liverpool Exchange with Newcastle nor even a successor to the local trains which ran between Sowerby Bridge and Normanton. Today, if you want to make this journey, you must rely on three separate train services which don't connect very well. In practice anyone travelling from Sowerby Bridge or Halifax to Wakefield or Normanton would go via Leeds and not attempt the journey I am making today.

There are only two scheduled passenger trains per day direct from Sowerby Bridge to Mirfield. Most journeys over this stretch of the Calder Valley are from Halifax to Huddersfield.

I'm on the 9.01 from New Pudsey to Huddersfield. It is eight minutes late but that can be recovered courtesy of the standing time at Bradford and Halifax. I'm bouncing along on a class 144. Each of the three carriages with bus seats is carried on only four wheels. It is all right for short journeys. Almost everyone but me alights at Halifax where a fresh handful of passengers get on. Last time I counted 15, it is slightly better today. Two ladies opposite are going shopping to Meadowhall – a half hour wait in Huddersfield then over an hour on another train like this one.

We only get a yellow signal to leave Halifax. This is because of approach control at Dryclough Junction where the speed limit for Huddersfield is lower than for Manchester. We proceed cautiously down the 1 in 44 through the 91 yard twin tunnel at Salterhebble. We cross the canal and river by a viaduct then curve sharply

into the Calder Valley main line at Greetland. Here the station and goods yard are long demolished. An oil tanker siding is in place but disused. The brick signal box was reopened in May 2000. There is no visible sign of the Stainland branch diverging to the right. It is far too overgrown. The same goes for many of the other branches which used to join, leave and cross our route.

Trains illustrated (November and December 1955 and January 1956) carries a contemporary description of the Calder Valley right through from Normanton to Manchester Victoria. It reads very different from the scene today. It is not just the railway which has changed but the industrial surroundings.

A viaduct takes us over the Calder. Then we go under the Elland bypass just yards before entering the 420 yard Elland Tunnel. Emerging back into daylight, we pass the site of Elland Station. The large low brick/wood signal box has plenty of white (=spare) levers. We cross two further viaducts before passing the lowfields development built on land vacated by the old power station.

The approach to Brighouse is over a viaduct then through the remains of the old station platforms until we come to a stand in the new structure, opened in May 2000. Less than half a dozen join here. There are a few more waiting on the other side for the Halifax train. The information screens seem to be working today. These are vital at an unstaffed station.

There used to be extensive sidings on the left hand side leaving Brighouse. From here to Wakefield there were four tracks but these have been reduced to two

Ivatt 2-6-2T No. 41253, based at Low Moor shed, pulls out of Greetland with a Huddersfield to Bradford local on 14 July 1959.
(G.W. Morrison)

Modernisation came too late to save Elland Station which closed within months of the introduction of 'Calder Valley' sets on the York to Sowerby Bridge service in 1962.
(Peter Sunderland)

Brighouse for Rastrick looking east. *(B.C. Lane collection)*

as far as Horbury Junction. There is no sign of Anchor Pit Junction, where the most direct line from Bradford trailed in. It was near to the massive motorway bridge. Approaching Bradley Wood Junction, we cross over onto the up line then curve away to the right on single track.

Today we are lucky and are not held by signals waiting to get out onto the main line at Bradley. We proceed along the ex LNWR route over which the Lancashire & Yorkshire had running powers into Huddersfield Station. Thanks to the slack schedule, we arrive early despite the late start. There is plenty of time to admire the magnificent station facade, recently enhanced by a statute of Harold Wilson, before joining the 10.38 to Wakefield.

This is a First North Western train, through from Manchester Victoria to Wakefield Westgate via Stalybridge. It is a two coach class 150 recently reliveried in dark blue and refurbished internally. The carriages are mounted on bogies and have train seats, a distinct grade up from the class 144 which has just set off back to Halifax and Bradford.

We rejoin the Calder Valley route by a burrowing junction at Heaton Lodge. We achieve this by using the first 1/4 mile of the 'Leeds New Line' described in *The Leeds Huddersfield & Manchester Railway*. Between 1970 and 1988, traffic towards Huddersfield also used the dive under but now up trains simply branch off by a flat junction.

As a result of the 1988 remodelling there are now three tracks between Heaton Lodge and Thornhill LNW Junctions, Mirfield engine shed still stands as a road tanker depot. The island platform at Mirfield

Station has been shortened. A badly kept garden occupies the base of what was the main building. A third platform appeared in 1990 on the up loop line. This is used by almost all up stopping trains (towards Manchester) rather than the south face of the island through which expresses pass.

Most passenger traffic takes the Leeds line at Thornhill LNW Junction. Immediately beyond, on the Leeds line only, are the platforms of Ravensthorpe & Thornhill Station. The L & Y had its own separate stations at Ravensthorpe, on the Cleckheaton branch, and Thornhill where that branch joins our route. Originally the station for Dewsbury, Thornhill closed at the end of 1961. The last station master was Frank Kipling whom I was fortunate to interview at his home in Thornhill in 1993. (see *The Great Northern Railway in the West Riding*).

The abutments can be seen of the bridge once carrying the Midland Railway Dewsbury Savile Town branch over our line. Then comes Dewsbury West Junction where the branch left for Dewsbury Market Place. Today West Junction is severed but cement wagons can be seen beyond buffer stops. They have to go round the triangular junction to join the main line at Dewsbury East Junction. The cement sidings are also the base of RMS Locotech which maintains private sidings in various parts of the country, also restoring diesel locomotives for hire to those sidings.

Thornhill Midland Junction came straight after Dewsbury East but on the other side. At this point the up and down Calder Valley lines part company to enclose the substantial marshalling yard at Healey Mills. This occupies a site stretching almost 1 1/2 miles

WD 2-8-0 No. 90710 heads a train of coal empties past Heaton Lodge in May 1966.   *(Peter Sunderland)*

31270 leaving Healey Mills yard, eastbound on 15 October 1981. *(Tom Heavyside)*

although the area nearest Thornhill is now just wasteland. At its opening on 23 July 1963, Healey Mills was capable of handling up to 4,500 wagons per day. It replaced 13 separate yards including a smaller one on the same site. Both the railway and the River Calder were diverted during construction of the complex which still includes a diesel depot and power signal box. A small part of the yard is still used for stabling through freight trains, also for civil engineers' traffic. The main purpose of this 1960s showpiece was quickly lost with the demise of wagonload freight – that is traffic in less than full train loads.

We rejoin the up line at what was Horbury & Ossett Station. Then comes the severed junction with the Barnsley branch before a deep rock cutting in which Horbury Millfield Road Station used to be found. Originally there was a 128 yard tunnel in this section. It was opened out when the line was quadrupled in 1903.

The other leg of the Barnsley branch curves in alongside a dam at Horbury Junction. In the angle of this junction, with rail access from the branch, is the Bombardier works which manufactures wagons, refurbishes passenger coaches and is now assembling most of the 'Virgin Voyager' cross country trains. The track remains quadruple from Horbury Junction into Wakefield Kirkgate. We pass under the long viaduct carrying the electrified main line into Wakefield Westgate. A single track comes down from Westgate to join us on the left. As we pull into Wakefield Kirkgate, the conductor announces that London passengers should stay on until Westgate to which the train will now reverse direction.

Anyone preferring to travel the last bit of the Calder Valley route to Normanton will have to alight at Wakefield Kirkgate. We are on platform 1 adjoining the long, disused facade at this large unstaffed station. A subway leads to the island platform 2 and 3. The high retaining wall confirms that there used to be an overall roof. Dilapidated canopies still hang over platform 3, also covering part of platform 2 which was outside the roof.

The train for Normanton is not until 11.56. It is the hourly all stations from Sheffield to Leeds via Barnsley and Castleford, formed of a three car class 144. Immediately out of Kirkgate is Wakefield East Junction where the Pontefract line diverges. Standing in the angle of this junction is Wakefield Kirkgate signalbox, a portakabin surmounted by a canopy. A triangle is completed by the Pontefract line curving back in at Turners Lane Junction. Carriage sidings used to occupy the triangle which is now overgrown. The countryside between Wakefield and Normanton is now green rather than black, the coal slag heaps having been landscaped.

The Calder Valley Line ends at Goose Hill Junction where it used to meet the Midland Main Line, 1/2 mile short of Normanton. Goose Hill is a junction no more. Traffic from Sheffield to Leeds uses other routes and parts of the Midland main line have been abandoned. Normanton Station reflects this loss of status. The large island platform structure is demolished except for a small section at the north end which has been retained to make today's modest unstaffed facility. Also swept away are the acres of sidings which used to occupy land to the west of the station.

L&Y 0-8-0 No. 201, built 1901, passing Healey Mills East Box about 1923. The splitting distants are for Horbury Station Junction where, the Barnsley branch diverges beyond Horbury & Ossett.
(Martin Bairstow collection)

Horbury Millfield Road, which opened in 1927, looking towards Wakefield. *(G.C. Lewthwaite)*

Horbury Junction Station, which was replaced by Millfield Road when the route was quadrupled.
(B.C. Lane collection)

Wakefield Kirkgate, still with overall roof, looking towards Mirfield in February 1967. 8F No. 48266 is approaching on the middle road.
(John Holroyd)

'Standard' 4-6-0 No. 75064 standing at Normanton.
(J.C.W. Halliday)

47483 passing Normanton on 7 May 1983 with a diverted Newcastle to Liverpool service. All that now remains is a short section of the island platform at the far end reached by a crossing over the up line instead of the footbridge. *(Tom Heavyside)*

Building the Calder Valley Main Line

The first serious step towards a railway between Manchester and Leeds was made in 1825 when George Stephenson recommended a route parallel to the Rochdale Canal. Entry into Yorkshire would be through a 1½ mile tunnel at Summit. Then the railway would run through the Calder Valley to a point near Brighouse from where it was to proceed to Leeds via Low Moor and the outskirts of Bradford.

A bill was presented to Parliament in 1831 for the Manchester to Sowerby Bridge section, the extension to Leeds being postponed for the time being. The bill was lost by the intervention of a general election called as part of the constitutional crisis preceding the 1832 Reform Act. The following year another attempt was frustrated by determined opposition from landowners and from the Rochdale Canal Company.

By the time of the next application to Parliament in 1836, Stephenson had recommended a longer but much easier route between Sowerby Bridge and Leeds following the Calder Valley through Wakefield to Normanton where connection was to be made with the proposed North Midland Railway from Derby to Leeds with which Stephenson was also associated. Opposition was overcome and the Manchester & Leeds Railway Act was passed on 4 July 1836.

The authorised route extended 51 miles from its terminal at Oldham Road, Manchester to a junction with the North Midland at Goose Hill south of Normanton. Running powers were granted over nine miles of the North Midland Railway to Leeds with the provision that powers to build this route would transfer to the Manchester & Leeds Railway if the North Midland fell down on the task.

Contracts were let from the Summer of 1837 commencing on the Lancashire side. Work proceeded sufficiently well to permit formal opening of the Manchester to Littleborough section on Wednesday 3 July 1839. A public service began the following day serving intermediate stations at Mills Hill (the nearest point to both Oldham and Middleton), Blue Pits (later named Castleton) and Rochdale.

Opening took place between Normanton and Hebden Bridge on 5 October 1840. Trains ran to and from Leeds over the North Midland Railway which had opened on 1 July that year. The North Midland provided the trains to work the Hebden Bridge service during the five months that it remained isolated from the Lancashire operation by incomplete works between Hebden Bridge and Littleborough.

It had been intended to build a 250 yard long tunnel at Charlestown, near Eastwood, but the hillside was not stable enough and in June 1840 the tunnel was found to be collapsing. It was decided to bypass it and the resultant Charlestown Curve was laid. Trains were then able to reach the east end of Summit Tunnel from 31 December. A stage coach provided the connection to Littleborough pending completion of the tunnel which was delayed a further two months.

The last brick was keyed in by the assistant engineer, Bernard Dickinson, on 11 December. According to the Manchester Guardian 'Gentlemen of the first respectability accompanied by a number of ladies were seen with lighted torches advancing towards the place to witness the ceremony of the completion of this great work'. Dickinson claimed that the tunnel 'defies the rage of tempest, fire or war or wasting age'. Unfortunately an invert failed causing damage which delayed the opening until 1 March 1841.

On 21 December 1840, a party of invited guests travelled from Manchester to Leeds walking through the tunnel. At the subsequent banquet in Leeds, George Stephenson commented on delays in getting the tunnel finished but offered some words of reassurance. 'I will stake my character, my head, if that tunnel ever give wa so as to bring danger to any of the public passing through. I don't think there is such another piece of wor in existence in the world'.

Manchester Victoria Station

The opening of the Summit tunnel created a continuous railway from Liverpool to Hull except for the break between Liverpool Road and Oldham Road stations in Manchester. Agreement was reached with the Liverpoo Manchester Railway that both lines would be extended t meet at Hunts Bank. By an Act of July 1839 the Manchester & Leeds Railway was authorised to constru a line from Miles Platting to Hunts Bank. This came into use on 1 January 1844, approaching Manchester down a in 47 incline on which for a short time rope working was used. From ¼ mile outside Victoria, ascending trains, hauled by their locomotive, were assisted from behind b a brake van which was attached to the rope. In the othe direction, trains descended by gravity but were controlle from the aforementioned brake van which had been attached to the front of the train at Miles Platting. By th summer of 1845 locomotives were working Miles Plattin 'bank' without assistance.

The station at Hunts Bank was named Manchester Victoria. Initially it had a single through platform 852 fee long with one bay at each end. The overall roof spanned the platform for most of its length. As traffic expanded the accommodation became inadequate and the station was enlarged progressively, the first extension coming in 1855 with the opening of suburban platforms for trains t Oldham, Stalybridge and Middleton.

Two new platforms were opened for main line trains in 1865 but were swept away when the station was rebuilt the late 1870s. A new suburban section with five platforms opened in November 1877. Reconstruction of the main line station with six through platforms was completed in 1884.

At the same time the London & North Western Railway, which as successor to the Liverpool & Manchester had hitherto shared Victoria, transferred its services to its own adjacent Exchange Station. LNWR trains from Leeds via Standedge passed through Victoria on the centre tracks between platforms 11 and 12 in orde to reach Exchange.

Victoria Station reached its fullest extent in 1904 when the number of platforms in the suburban station was increased to ten. In 1930, platform 11 at Victoria, which on the original 1844 site was extended to join platform 3 at Exchange, the combined length of 2,238 feet making i the longest in Europe. In 1969 Exchange closed and services reverted to Victoria to the greater convenience o passengers.

The West Riding Lines

Between Sowerby Bridge and Leeds the Manchester & Leeds Railway encircled but went little way to serve the heavy woollen district of Yorkshire. Stations at Elland fo Halifax, Brighouse for Bradford, Cooper Bridge for Huddersfield and Thornhill for Dewsbury could not put o indefinitely the aspirations of these towns for a direct service. A branch to Halifax was authorised in 1839 but work did not commence until 1843. In 1¾ miles from a junction at North Dean (later known as Greetland), the

The goods offices at Manchester Oldham Road built 1913-14 at the original Manchester & Leeds Railway terminus. *(John Marshall)*

An Aspinall 4-4-2 on Luddendenfoot troughs with an eastbound express shortly before 1914.
(B.C. Lane collection)

The booking office at the original 1844 Halifax Station.
(Martin Bairstow collection)

single track climbed 144 feet with a maximum gradient of 1 in 44½ and crossed the River Calder by an iron bridge of four spans. The terminus was at Shaw Syke, a little short of the later station right at the bottom of the town. The line opened on 1 July 1844.

At this time work was beginning on the Leeds & Bradford Railway which connected those two cities by the so called 'valley' route via Shipley which had been favoured by Stephenson but which had faced opposition from exponents of a shorter, more steeply graded, alternative via Stanningley. The Leeds & Bradford Railway had secured its Act only after giving a number of promises about extensions, one of which was to continue the line from its terminus at Bradford (the present Forster Square) through Halifax to meet the Manchester & Leeds near Sowerby Bridge. The Leeds & Bradford was part of the 'Empire' of George Hudson and was expected to be merged with the Midland Railway. The Manchester & Leeds put forward counter proposals by promoting the Leeds & West Riding Junction Railway to which it was to subscribe half the capital, the rest being found locally. A comprehensive network was proposed to serve the woollen district including a line from Sowerby Bridge via Halifax and Low Moor to Leeds, with a branch from Low Moor to Bradford, a line from the Calder Valley near Dewsbury through Cleckheaton to Low Moor and one from Dewsbury to Leeds via Batley. By either Low Moor or Batley the distance between Manchester and Leeds would be shortened by about 12 miles compared to the route via Normanton.

Arguments between the two rival schemes included the question of whether a train could climb from the low lying Leeds & Bradford terminus towards Low Moor without rope assistance. Supporters of the Manchester & Leeds said it couldn't. Their route would not face that problem since having climbed from Leeds to Laisterdyke it would stay at that height to Low Moor, leaving Bradford to be served by a branch which would not descend to quite as low an altitude as the Leeds & Bradford station. Supporters of the Leeds – Bradford 'short line' favoured the Manchester & Leeds proposal since a branch from Laisterdyke to Bradford would achieve their goal. In Halifax there was some support for the Leeds & Bradford Railway whose extension to Sowerby Bridge would serve their town. They suspected that the Manchester & Leeds might concentrate on the Dewsbury – Leeds and Dewsbury – Cleckheaton – Bradford lines, thus leaving Halifax with just its branch line from North Dean and bypassed by the main lines.

Both schemes went to Parliament in 1845 and both were rejected following which the rival parties then got together. Despite Hudson's connection with the Midland it was agreed in November 1845 that the Leeds & Bradford and Manchester & Leeds Railways should amalgamate and that various new lines should be promoted under the title of the West Riding Union Railways. An Act of 18 August 1846, authorised a railway from Sowerby Bridge via Halifax, Low Moor and Stanningley to Leeds, with a branch from Bowling to join the Leeds & Bradford Railway at Bradford together with lines from Mirfield to Low Moor, from Elland to Huddersfield and from Wyke to Brighouse.

On 30 June 1846, the day the Leeds & Bradford Railway opened, Hudson offered to lease it to the Midland having broken off the agreement to amalgamate with the Manchester & Leeds. Plans for connecting the West Riding Union lines with the Leeds & Bradford were soon dropped and when the former reached Bradford in 1850 it terminated at what became the Exchange Station leaving Bradford to this day with two dead end stations and no link between them.

Powers to build the railway from Thornhill to Leeds via Batley had been granted by Parliament to the Leeds, Dewsbury & Manchester Railway. The line opened on 18 September 1848 and was used by the Manchester & Leeds for the next six years as it was so much shorter than the Normanton route. However, the M&L, which changed its name to the Lancashire & Yorkshire Railway in 1847, forewent the opportunity to purchase the Dewsbury line allowing it to become part of the London & North Western Railway's Leeds to Manchester route via Standedge Tunnel.

Meanwhile the L&Y pressed on with its West Riding lines. The first part to be opened in 1848 was from Mirfield to Low Moor via the Spen Valley (described later). On 22 March 1850, amid due ceremony, the last stone was keyed into the Moorish arch at the Low Moor end of Bowling Tunnel and the biggest obstacle to reaching Bradford had been overcome. The 3 miles from Low Moor to Bradford opened 9 May 1850, terminating at "an elevated point near the Court House where a neat and commodious station has been erected". Bradford was now connected with Manchester, but only via Mirfield. Another three months saw the opening of the Low Moor to Halifax link on 7 August. The *Bradford Observer* commented "verily Halifax and Bradford have no excuse for being strangers". At Halifax a temporary wooden structure was opened at the bottom of Horton Street about ¼ mile nearer to Bradford than the previous terminus at Shaw Syke and Horton Street remains the location of Halifax station to the present day. A permanent structure completed in 1855 had two platforms but by the 1880s was grossly inadequate and a new station was opened in 1885/6. Built by the Lancashire & Yorkshire and Great Northern Railways this had three island platforms and was approached by a road bridge which spanned the goods lines.

The West Riding lines so far constructed had consumed more capital than expected and only one more was built. On 1 January 1852, the direct link opened between Milner Royd Junction, near Sowerby Bridge, and Dryclough Junction from where the previous single track branch into Halifax was doubled.

The Leeds, Bradford & Halifax Junction Railway

Unable to finance further work on the West Riding lines, the L&Y sought powers of abandonment. In the case of the route between Bradford and Leeds via Stanningley, an independent company was immediately formed to fill the breach. The Leeds, Bradford & Halifax Junction Railway was incorporated on 30 June 1852, the Act providing for a reciprocal exchange of running powers for the L&Y between Bowling Junction and Leeds and for the LB&HJ from Bowling to Halifax. A further Act dated 4 August 1853, authorised a branch from Laisterdyke to Bradford and provided for the LB&HJ to be worked by the Great Northern Railway. Work was completed speedily and the railway opened on 1 August 1854. The L&Y immediately diverted its Leeds traffic this way and ceased to use the LNWR route through Dewsbury.

Bradford was served by three railways each with its own terminus. In 1864 a line was authorised from Hammerton Street to Mill Lane Junction to give Great Northern trains access to the L&Y station where an additional platform was provided. The new arrangements were completed on 7 January 1867, allowing the closure of Bradford Adolphus Street to passenger traffic. The GNR had absorbed the LB&HJ Railway on 5 September 1865.

The introduction of GN trains, together with a general

The pre 1876 station at Sowerby Bridge.

(John Marshall collection)

Halifax Station in August 1912 with a 4-6-0 leaving on the 1.10 pm Bradford to Manchester Express which on Wednesdays and Saturdays ran independently of the Leeds to Liverpool seen in the adjacent platform. On the extreme left is the 1.58 NER train to Hull which ran via Cleckheaton.

(National Railway Museum)

increase in traffic, put great pressure on the capacity at Bradford Exchange which was approached by a double track tunnel and was soon to prove a bottleneck. Incoming GN trains had to cross the paths of departing L&Y trains at Mill Lane Junction, whilst all shunting movements out of the station involved entering the tunnel which was on a 1 in 50 gradient. Plans were made to open out the tunnel and quadruple the track and in 1876 a bridge was completed just below Mill Lane Junction carrying Caledonia Street over the railway instead of by a level crossing. A goods yard was built at Bridge Street on the west side of the station so as to release the earlier yard for enlargement of the passenger station. A new 10 platform terminus was completed in 1888 with separate halves for GN and L&Y trains, each of which had its own pair of tracks for Mill Lane Junction.

Stations in Leeds
The first terminus in Leeds used by the Manchester & Leeds Railway was at Hunslet Lane situated to the south of the City centre and shared with the Midland Railway. In 1846 the Midland transferred most of its services to the centrally situated Wellington Station which was built by the Leeds & Bradford Railway.

The Manchester & Leeds Railway stayed at Hunslet Lane after 1846 but diverted most of its trains via the LNWR route through Batley in 1848. This crossed over the Midland Leeds & Bradford line at Holbeck and terminated at a temporary station, about 1/4 mile from Wellington, near the site of Leeds Central where the permanent structure was opened about 1851. The Leeds, Bradford & Halifax Junction Railway also ran into Leeds Central. A two level station was opened at Holbeck in 1855 to permit interchange between the GNR and the North Eastern Leeds – Harrogate trains below.

The present passenger station is the one opened in 1869 by the London & North Western and North Eastern Railways called Leeds New. In 1938 New and Wellington were joined together and renamed Leeds City. In 1967 Leeds Central Station was closed and services transferred to Leeds City. Trains from Bradford Exchange now join the former Midland line at Whitehall Junction.

Heaton Lodge Junction
The trans-Pennine monopoly of the Lancashire & Yorkshire Railway was broken with the completion of the alternative route via Standedge Tunnel and Huddersfield in 1849. This route, which became part of the London & North Western Railway, utilised the L&Y in the Calder Valley between Heaton Lodge and Thornhill LNW Junctions. The Standedge route was promoted by two companies: the Huddersfield & Manchester and the Leeds, Dewsbury & Manchester. It had been thought that the new railway would have an independent route through Mirfield but since there was little chance of the L&Y preventing the new line, which was so much shorter than its own, a compromise was sought involving an exchange of running powers. The L&Y did not oppose the Standedge route nor the amalgamation of the two promoting companies with the LNWR. In return the LNWR dropped opposition to the L&Y West Riding lines, provided that a branch from Cooper Bridge to Huddersfield was abandoned. The LNWR gained running powers over the Calder Valley line from Heaton Lodge Junction to Thornhill whilst the L&Y was allowed access into Huddersfield from Heaton Lodge and Bradley Wood.

The railway from Heaton Lodge to Huddersfield opened on 3 August 1847, followed by that from Thornhill to Leeds on 18 September 1848. The curve from Bradley Wood to Bradley, which permitted a Halifax to Huddersfield service was opened by the LNWR on 1 January 1852.

In 1884 the three mile stretch between Heaton Lodge and Thornhill LNW Junction became the first section of the Calder Valley line to be quadrupled although the Calder bridge at Mirfield was not widened until 1932. A further measure of relief was afforded to this congested route when the LNWR opened its Leeds 'New Line' in 1900. From Spen Valley Junction, just south of Heaton Lodge, this passed under the Calder Valley line and provided a route from Huddersfield to Leeds which did not conflict with L&Y traffic. In 1932 a colour light signalling system was introduced between Heaton Lodge and Thornhill which indicated the speed at which trains were to pass over junctions. This gave way to standard BR power signalling in 1970 when the area controlled by Healey Mills power box was extended to join with fringe boxes at Huddersfield, Elland and Batley. The Leeds 'New Line' closed in 1965, but the track from Spen Valley Junction under the main line was retained and used to form a dive-under to allow passenger trains from Huddersfield to Leeds to avoid conflicting with freight traffic on the Sowerby Bridge to Wakefield route.

With the decline in freight after 1970, the dive under became unnecessary in that form. In 1988 it was remodelled into the present burrowing junction with only the down line (from Huddersfield) diving under the Calder Valley tracks.

Developments in Lancashire
The Manchester & Leeds Railway had opened a branch from Miles Platting to Stalybridge in 1846. LNWR trains by the Standedge route left Manchester Victoria and travelled over L&Y tracks as far as Stalybridge and this meant that from 1849 both Trans-Pennine routes were using Miles Platting bank imposing strain on the capacity of the double track over that section. The Manchester 'loop-line' was authorised by an Act of 1872 to enable the bulk of L&Y traffic to avoid Miles Platting. The four track 'loop-line' started immediately outside Victoria Station and extended 2 miles to rejoin the main line at Thorpes Bridge Junction 3/4 mile north of Miles Platting. The maximum gradient was 1 in 63 compared to 1 in 47 on the older route. Opened to goods on 29 October 1877, the 'loop line' was used by the majority of passenger trains to the Calder Valley from 1 August 1878. A new motive power depot opened at Newton Heath in 1876 to replace the facilities at Miles Platting where both running sheds and workshops had shared a rather cramped site between the Oldham Road and Victoria lines below Collyhurst Junction. In 1877 the carriage works were moved to a position on the north west of Thorpes Bridge Junction alongside the 'loop line'. Locomotive building and repair work continued at Miles Platting for another 10 years until this was transferred to the new L&Y workshops at Horwich. Miles Platting works were partly demolished in the building of the line between Brewery Sidings and New Allen Street Junction which provided a direct link from the Calder Valley route to Oldham Road goods depot by means of a flyover across Miles Platting bank. Opened in 1890, this new facility improved access to the goods depot and avoided conflicting movement with LNWR and L&Y passenger trains into Victoria. Additional stations were opened at Smithy Bridge in 1868 and at Moston in 1872. The build up of local services put pressure on the facilities at Rochdale where a new station was completed in 1891, consisting of two large island platforms with a double track bay at the Manchester end of the up platform and a similar bay at the opposite end of the Leeds bound platform.

A class 40 emerges from Summit Tunnel and is about to pass through the short Summit West bore.

(R.S. Greenwood)

Robinson class 04 2-8-0s regularly ran from the east as far as Elland Power Station but their appearances further west were much less frequent. 63766 passing Summit East signal box with a train of coal on 6 May 1960.

(R.S. Greenwood)

Widening the Main Line

From 1876 Parliamentary approval was sought to install four tracks over various sections of the line from Manchester to Normanton. The ultimate aim was to widen the line throughout, but this was never completed partly due to the physical difficulty of laying four tracks in the upper Calder Valley and also due to the intervention of the First World War. The following sections were increased to four tracks over the period to 1914 generally by the provision of goods loops between stations:

Manchester Victoria to Moston Colliery Sidings
Middleton Junction to Mills Hill
Castleton Sidings to Rochdale
Littleborough to Summit West
Todmorden to Hall Royd Junction
Hebden Bridge to Mytholmroyd West
Mytholmroyd East to Luddendenfoot
Brighouse to Horbury & Ossett
Horbury Junction to Wakefield Kirkgate

In addition there were goods loops on both sides at Vitriol Works, Smithy Bridge, Sowerby Bridge and Elland, whilst at Eastwood there were two loops on the Manchester bound side. At Brighouse a new station opened on 1 May 1893, nearer to Manchester on the section which remained double track so that the site of the old station could be taken up by the additional lines. The stations at Mirfield, Thornhill and Horbury & Ossett each had island platforms on the northernmost pair of tracks which were known as the 'slow' lines.

The scheme for widening throughout from Todmorden to Brighouse would have involved new tunnels at Castle Hill, Horsfall, Weasel Hall, Sowerby Bridge and Elland. Millwood would have been opened out. This work was never started and in 1916 plans for a new station at Mytholmroyd were abandoned so that the four track section between Hebden Bridge and Luddendenfoot remained confined to two tracks only through Mytholmroyd Station. In 1927 the LMS completed the widening of its Horbury to Wakefield section and this involved the opening out of Horbury Tunnel and the filling in of a 16 arch viaduct west of Wakefield. The station at Horbury Junction was very inconveniently situated and, rather than rebuild it to suit the new track layout, a new station was opened at Horbury Millfield Road, nearer to the town centre. The arrangement of the four tracks from Horbury Station Junction (where the Barnsley line diverges at Horbury & Ossett) to Wakefield Kirkgate was different to the section west of Horbury. The two eastbound tracks and two westbound tracks were each paired together with the 'fast' lines in the middle so that trains stopping at both Millfield Road and Horbury & Ossett Stations had to switch from fast to slow lines or vice versa at Horbury Station Junction. Through Horbury & Ossett Station there were a total of six tracks, the four main line ones being supplemented on the outside by goods loops in each direction. When the new marshalling yard was being built at Healey Mills in the early 1960s the arrangement of tracks previously in use between Wakefield and Horbury Station Junction was extended to Thornhill Midland Junction so that the new yard was enclosed by the two eastbound tracks on one side and the two westbound tracks on the other. The arrangement of platforms and tracks at Horbury & Ossett Station became the same as Millfield Road with the island platform serving the centre 'fast' lines. After 1965 the widened sections were reduced back to double track.

The only quadruple sections remaining in 2000 are from Manchester Victoria to Miles Platting and from Horbury Junction to Wakefield Kirkgate.

Aspinall 4-4-0 No. 1227, with a westbound express between Mytholmroyd and Hebden Bridge. Built in 1894, this engine survived as LMS No. 10172 until 1925.

(B. C. Lane collection)

The four track section of the Leeds, Bradford & Halifax Junction line between Bramley and Holbeck, widened in the 1890s, reverted to double track in 1968.

The Midland West Riding Lines

In 1898 the Midland Railway was authorised to build a cut off to its Anglo Scottish main line from Royston to Bradford. Shorter than the route via Leeds, the scheme would open up the West Riding towns to the Midland and also provide a through route for Bradford. Plans for duplicating lines in the Calder and Spen Valleys were abandoned in return for running powers over L&Y routes. The tracks from Royston to Thornhill Midland Junction opened to goods traffic on 10 November 1905, and the L&Y Railway began a Halifax to Sheffield passenger service over it in 1909. A branch from Mirfield to a Midland Railway goods depot at Huddersfield Newtown opened in 1910 but this never carried a passenger service. Likewise the branch into Dewsbury Saville Town which crossed over the Calder Valley near Thornhill failed to develop as planned.

The part of the Midland scheme which would have radically altered the pattern of railway operation in West Yorkshire was the proposed link from the L&Y Spen Valley line north of Cleckheaton across Bradford with high level platforms at Forster Square then descending to join the existing route at Manningham. The project was overtaken by the First World War. The Thornhill to Royston Section closed in 1968 having seen little use by passenger trains since 1916.

Thornhill No. 1 box seen from a train which is about to join the Calder Valley Main Line from the Spen Valley branch. *(J.C.W. Halliday)*

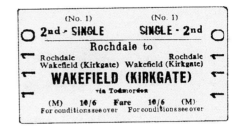

Fairburn 2-6-4T No. 42107 leaving Leeds Central with the 12.55 to Liverpool Exchange on 23 September 1960. *(G.W. Morrison)*

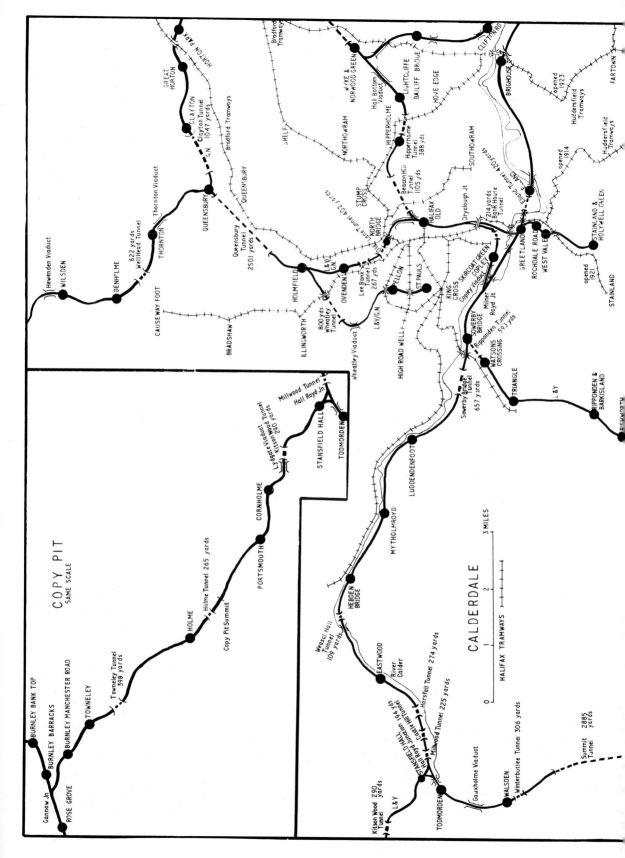

HORTON PARK

GREAT HORTON

CLAYTON TUNNEL
Clayton Tunnel
G.N. 1047 yards

Bradford Tramways

QUEENSBURY

Bradford Tramways

CLIFTON RD

WYKE & NORWOOD GREEN

NORWOOD GREEN

LIGHTCLIFFE

BAILIFF BRIDGE

Hall Bottom Viaduct

HOVE EDGE

BRIGHOUSE

opened 1923

FARTOWN

Huddersfield Tramways

HIPPERHOLME

Hipperholme Tunnel 388 yds

opened 1914

Huddersfield Tramways

opened 1921

STAINLAND

STAINLAND & HOLYWELL GREEN

NORTHOWRAM

SOUTHOWRAM

HemmelField Tunnel 402 yards

Beacon Hill Tunnel 1105 yds

HALIFAX OLD

Dryclough Jt

214 yds
Bank House Tunnel

GREETLAND

ROCHDALE ROAD

WEST VALE

STUMP CROSS

SHELF

THORNTON

Thornton Viaduct

622 yards Wellhead Tunnel

WILSDEN

Hewenden Viaduct

DENHOLME

CAUSEWAY FOOT

Queensbury Tunnel 2501 yards

HOLMFIELD

ILLINGWORTH

BRADSHAW

800 yds Wheatley Tunnel

OVENDEN

Lee Bank Tunnel 267 yds

L&Y/G.N.

L&Y/G.N.

NORTH BRIDGE

L&Y/G.N.

Wheatley Viaduct

PELLON

ST PAULS

HIGH ROAD WELL

KING CROSS

SKIRCOAT GREEN

Copley Viaduct

COPLEY

SOWERBY BRIDGE

Milner Royd Jt

Ripponden Tunnel 593 yds

WATSONS CROSSING

TRIANGLE

L&Y

RIPPONDEN & BARKISLAND

Sowerby Bridge Tunnel 657 yards

RISHWORTH

COPY PIT
SAME SCALE

BURNLEY BANK TOP

BURNLEY BARRACKS

BURNLEY MANCHESTER ROAD

TOWNELEY

Towneley Tunnel 398 yards

Gannow Jn

ROSE GROVE

HOLME

Holme Tunnel 265 yards

Copy Pit Summit

PORTSMOUTH

CORNHOLME

Lydgate Viaduct Tunnel Kitson Wood Tunnel 290 yards

STANSFIELD HALL

Millwood Tunnel Hall Royd Jn

TODMORDEN

LUDDENDENFOOT

MYTHOLMROYD

HEBDEN BRIDGE

Wessel Hall Tunnel 109 yards

EASTWOOD

River Calder

Horsfall Tunnel 274 yards

Millwood Tunnel 225 yards

STANSFIELD HALL Junction
Hall Royd Junction

Castle Hill Tunnel 194 yds

Kitson Wood 290 yards

TODMORDEN

L&Y

Gauxholme Viaduct

WALSDEN

Winterbutlee Tunnel 306 yards

Summit Tunnel 2885 yards

CALDERDALE

HALIFAX TRAMWAYS

0   1   2   3 MILES

34

Train Services

The Early Years

The first passenger service offered by the Manchester & Leeds Railway in 1839 was ten trains each way daily (four on Sundays) from Manchester Oldham Road to Littleborough. For the short time that the Leeds – Hebden Bridge service operated as an isolated line it had no Sunday service but once opened throughout the trains ran seven days per week, a controversial step in those days. The timetable reproduced below operated during the first half of 1844, after the extension to Victoria but before the Halifax branch opened. In addition to first and second class carriages, many of the trains conveyed 'Stanhopes' which were 17 ft long open trucks with no seats, but divided into four compartments by longitudinal and latitudinal bars. "The desire evinced by your directors to properly afford the poorer classes of the district the conveniences of third class travelling has resulted in a due appreciation of the boon conferred. The plan adopted is to run one or more carriages of that description with every train." Lest third class passengers found the going too easy, an edict was issued that "the Company's servants are strictly ordered not to porter for wagon passengers".

Thomas Normington, who worked for the Lancashire & Yorkshire Railway from 1847 until 1895 and wrote a book on his retirement, recalls his first railway journey which took place in 1845 from Dewsbury to Manchester. He travelled in a 'Stanhope' and on emerging from Summit Tunnel found himself somewhat dirty whilst his hat had been burned by a spark from the engine.

MANCHESTER & LEEDS RAILWAY

WEEKDAYS	am	am	am	am	am	pm	pm	pm	pm		SUNDAYS am	am	pm
MANCHESTER VIC		6 45		9 00	10 50	1 20	3 20	4 45	7 00		8 00	10 50	7 00
MILES PLATTING		6 48		9 03	10 53	1 23	3 23	4 48	7 03		8 03	10 53	7 03
MIDDLETON		7 02		9 20	–	1 40	3 36	5 00	7 20		8 20	11 05	7 20
BLUE PITS		7 14		9 30	11 15	1 54	3 58	5 15	7 34		8 38	11 15	7 38
ROCHDALE		7 20		9 37	11 22	2 02	4 08	5 22	7 44		8 48	11 22	7 48
LITTLEBOROUGH		7 28		9 45	–	2 12	4 16	–	7 56		8 56	–	7 56
TODMORDEN	5w30	7 47		10 10	11 42	2 30	4 32	5 42	8 16		9 13	11 42	8 13
EASTWOOD	5w34	–		10 14	–	2 34	4 36	–	8 20		9 17	–	8 17
HEBDEN BRIDGE	5w46	8 00	9 00	10 26	–	2 46	4 48	5 55	8 32		9 33	–	8 33
LUDDENDENFOOT	5w50	8 07	9 06	10 30	–	2 55	4 54	–	8 41		9 39	–	8 39
SOWERBY BRIDGE	6 00	8 12	9 14	10 39	12 08	3 01	5 02	6 08	8 49		9 47	12 08	8 47
ELLAND	6 09	8 20	9 24	10 50	12 13	3 11	5 11	6 13	8 59		9 57	12 13	8 57
BRIGHOUSE	6 19	8 35	9 36	11 02	12 21	3 24	5 19	6 21	9 12		10 05	12 21	9 05
COOPER BRIDGE	6 30	8 44	9 46	11 15	12 30	3 33	5 27	6 30	9 21		10 13	12 30	9 13
DEWSBURY	6 42	8 56	9 57	11 25	–	3 44	5 37	6 40	9 33		10 25	–	9 25
HORBURY	6 54	9 06	10 09	11 30	–	3 54	5 50	–	9 45		10 36	–	9 36
WAKEFIELD	7 06	9 17	10 20	11 50	12 53	4 05	6 02	6 53	9 57		10 50	12 53	9 50
NORMANTON	7 15	9 27	10 34	12 10	1 18	4 15	6 20	7 10	10 08		11 08	1 18	10 08
LEEDS HUNSLET LN	7 40	9 50	10 55	12 30	1 38	4 35	6 45	7 30	10 30		11 30	1 38	10 30

WEEKDAYS	am	am	am	am	am	pm	pm	pm	pm	pm	SUNDAYS am	am	pm
LEEDS HUNSLET LN	5 40		7 00	9 00	10 10		1 00	3 45	6 10	7 15	7 00	10 10	7 15
NORMANTON	6 00		7 30	9 20	10 35		1 30	4 10	6 30	7 40	7 26	10 35	7 41
WAKEFIELD	6 08		7 45	9 40	10 50		1 45	4 20	6 42	7 55	7 44	10 50	7 59
HORBURY	–		7 55	9 50	–		–	4 34	6 54	–	7 59	–	8 14
DEWSBURY	6 25		8 10	9 58	–		2 09	4 41	7 04	8 09	8 11	–	8 26
COOPER BRIDGE	6 40		8 24	10 07	11 13		2 24	4 50	7 16	8 18	8 26	11 13	8 41
BRIGHOUSE	6 50		8 34	10 13	11 23		2 34	5 00	7 26	8 28	8 36	11 23	8 51
ELLAND	7 00		8 45	10 25	11 35		2 45	5 10	7 34	8 35	8 47	11 35	9 02
SOWERBY BRIDGE	7 09		8 58	10 30	11 40		2 58	5 20	7 42	8 45	8 57	11 40	9 12
LUDDENDENFOOT	–		9 04	–	–		–	5 30	7 50	–	9 04	–	9 19
HEBDEN BRIDGE	7 18		9 12	10 45	–		3 11	5 45	8 02	8 59	9 12	–	9 27
EASTWOOD	7T32		9 24	–	–		–	–	–	–	9 26	–	9 41
TODMORDEN	7 38		9 30	11 10	12 10	2 00	3 27	6 05	8 22	9 15	9 32	12 10	9 47
LITTLEBOROUGH	7 54		9 50	–	–	2 18	–	6 19	8 36	–	9 48	–	10 03
ROCHDALE	8 03	9 15	10 00	11 32	12 30	2 30	3 57	6 32	8 42	9 37	9 58	12 32	10 13
BLUE PITS	8 10	9 22	10 07	11 40	–	2 38	4 05	6 40	–	–	10 06	–	10 21
MIDDLETON	8 20	9 30	10 15	11 46	12 40	2 50	4 15	6 45	8 58	–	10 20	12 44	10 35
MILES PLATTING	8 28	9 43	10 28	11 58	12 50	2 58	4 28	6 58	9 08	9 58	10 32	12 53	10 43
MANCHESTER VIC	8 30	9 45	10 30	12 00	12 52	3 00	4 30	7 00	9 10	10 00	10 35	12 55	10 45

OLDHAM BRANCH

FROM MANCHESTER	FROM OLDHAM
WEEKDAYS	
7 30am	8 00am
8 30	9 00
10 00	10 30
11 00	11 30
12 40pm	1 10pm
2 40	3 15
4 00	4 30
5 00	5 40
6 40	7 10
8 00	8 30
SUNDAYS	
7 40am	8 10am
10 10	11 00
1 00pm	1 30pm
2 30	3 00
6 30	7 00
7 30	8 00

A train will depart every weekday morning from the Oldham station at 6 50 to meet the 6 45 train from Manchester at Middleton station.

JANUARY 1844

T-TUESDAYS ONLY W-WEDNESDAYS ONLY

Very superior accomodation is afforded at the Normanton Hotel for those passengers or families wishing to go to London, York, Hull, Newcastle &c by the earliest trains. The 4 45 & 7 00 trains from Manchester, by remaining all night at Normanton, are peculiarly adapted for this purpose.

From 1847 to 1854 Manchester to Leeds trains made use of the London & North Western line from Thornhill LNW Junction to Leeds Central. 'Bradshaw' for November 1850 shows six trains leaving Leeds by this route and picking up either connections or through carriages from Normanton at Mirfield. Additionally two trains still departed from Leeds Hunslet Lane and ran to Manchester via Normanton, but these ceased at the end of February 1851 when Hunslet Lane closed as a passenger station. The line to Bradford had then been only recently opened and departures from that City consisted of nine trains to North Dean most of which offered connections to Manchester and one extra to Halifax. The fastest time from Manchester Victoria to Leeds Central was exactly two hours by the 5.45 pm which was first and second class only. The 'Parliamentary' services by which third class passengers now travelled in covered but spartan carriages were generally the first trains of the day.

When the direct line from Halifax to Sowerby Bridge opened on 1 January 1852, trains from Bradford were run to and from Sowerby Bridge instead of North Dean which was instead served by five trains per day between Halifax and Huddersfield via Bradley Wood Junction. With the opening of the Leeds, Bradford and Halifax Junction Railway in 1854 all Manchester to Leeds services were diverted via Halifax and Bowling and most trains detached Bradford carriages at Low Moor.

A Royal Visit

On 3 August 1863, the Prince of Wales arrived in Halifax to open the new Town Hall. In those day's such a visit would offer many people a very rare break from their normal working life and many would be given a days holiday. Thomas Normington was entrusted with the task of co-ordinating the special trains to Halifax which ran on Tuesday, 4 August from nearly every station in Yorkshire served by the L&Y and GN Railways. Halifax station had only two platforms and telegraph was only in partial use. The method was to keep trains on the move and not to terminate them at Halifax. Specials from Mirfield via Cleckheaton continued back to Mirfield via Brighouse and then went round again. Those from Todmorden worked through to Bradford and so on. Between 3 pm and midnight there were 114 ordinary and special trains booked to leave Halifax and it is claimed that some

125,000 passengers were carried. A temporary booking office was established at Halifax whilst the numbers of ticket collectors at various stations were reinforced so that all tickets could be collected at the last stop before Halifax. We do not know how many of the trains ran to time but the following extracts from the special traffic notice illustrate potential problems:

"The station masters at Sowerby Bridge and Low Moor Stations must use every exertion to keep the ordinary trains to time. Much depends on their skill and discretion in not allowing the special trains to leave their station when likely to be in the way to Halifax."

"The Great Northern company to have a spare engine at Halifax ready to hook on to every train arriving from Leeds or Wakefield and return with it at once. This is to prevent causing a block at the station. All GN trains returning will start from the goods siding calling at the station to take up passengers."

Services in 1910

The difficulty in describing the pattern of train services at this time is that they were so complicated. Departures were on anything but a regular interval basis. The first train from Normanton left at 3.22 am and ran via Greetland to Halifax where it connected with the 3.50 am from Leeds Central to Manchester Victoria. The first all stations Bradford to Halifax train departed at 5.15 am and amalgamated with the 4.55 from Leeds at Low Moor. 5.15 also saw the first all stations to Manchester train leave Littleborough. The first express from Leeds to Liverpool left at 9.16 am stopping at Holbeck, Stanningley, Low Moor and Halifax, where the Bradford portion was attached, then running non-stop to reach Manchester at

10.40 having slipped two coaches at Rochdale. It was followed out of Halifax by a slow train to Manchester which served every station as far as Castleton. Stations thence to Manchester had their own local service. Furth Liverpool expresses left Leeds Central at 9.55 and 11.00 whilst the 1.00 pm was advertised as a "vestibule luncheon car train" and reached Manchester in 1 hour 2 minutes with stops at Holbeck, Low Moor, Halifax, Sowerby Bridge and Todmorden. The "through dining train" at 12.30 pm from Newcastle to Liverpool took 4 hours 40 minutes throughout and ran non-stop from Wakefield to Manchester in 58 minutes. In so far as the was a pattern to the service, passengers could get from Leeds, Bradford or Wakefield to Manchester almost eve hour whilst the intermediate stations generally had train at least every two hours. Many of those in the West Riding and between Rochdale and Manchester were als served by local trains including those between Bradford and Huddersfield, between Bradford, Dewsbury and Wakefield and between Manchester, Middleton and Oldham which traversed sections of the Calder Valley Main Line.

The last through train of the day from Leeds Central was at 9.00 pm calling at Low Moor, to pick up the Bradford coaches, Halifax, Sowerby Bridge then all stations to Middleton Junction arriving Manchester Victoria at 10.56. There was a 9.40 pm from Normanton Manchester Victoria into which Bradford passengers co connect at Sowerby Bridge. This reached Manchester a 11.57 Mondays to Fridays but 12.04 am on Saturdays when it made more stops. The last train from Leeds to Sowerby Bridge left at 10.58 joining the 11.12 from Bradford at Low Moor. On Saturdays Only there was th

Passing Dryclough Junction, bound for Blackpool Central on 6 July 1963 is one of the class 110 sets, purpose built for the Calder Valley route in 1961. *(Martin Bairstow collection)*

An Aspinall 'Atlantic' in almost original condition pauses at Sowerby Bridge with a Manchester train about 1910.
(B.C. Lane collection)

Viewed from above the tunnel, a 2-6-4T has left Sowerby Bridge for Manchester. Loco shed to left, site of pre 1876 station to right. The 'new' station is out of sight in the distance.
(Peter Sunderland)

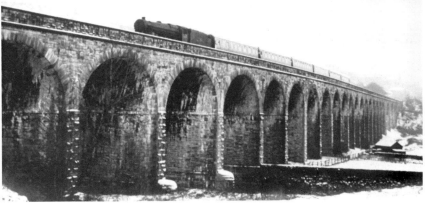

45219 crossing Copley Viaduct bound from Bradford to Blackpool on 31 December 1961, the day before dieselisation of the main Calder Valley passenger service.
(Martin Bairstow collection)

customary extra late train at 11.10 from Leeds and 11.30 from Bradford running semi fast to Manchester where arrival was at 12.56 am.

On Sundays, the service was more restricted with just six trains mostly slow from Leeds to Manchester, some involving changes at Sowerby Bridge. At 10.03 pm there was an all stations Leeds Central to Halifax operated by the GNR on the direct route via Stanningley and Low Moor.

Goods traffic was intense with vast quantities of coal from the Yorkshire coalfield to the woollen mills of Yorkshire and the Lancashire cotton towns. The finished products of these industries were conveyed by rail for both home and export markets and practically every station had its attendant goods depot. There were numerous private sidings whilst the L&Y established marshalling yards at Normanton and Healey Mills.

Diesel Services

British Railways embarked on its mass diesel multiple unit programme in 1954. The first route to be favoured with the new trains was the former Leeds, Bradford & Halifax Junction Railway. From June 1954 a half hourly service operated from Bradford Exchange to Leeds Central with hourly trains running through to Harrogate.

This first dmu service was a success, the number of passengers increasing four fold in as many years. According to the Assistant Operating Officer North Eastern Region 'An uplift in morale is noticeable wherever diesels have been introduced and a more brisk and business like attitude to train services is apparent. The public have responded to this first tangible result of the modernisation plan quickly and permanently and the impact of this new mode of travel is unmistakable' (*Trains Illustrated* January 1959).

Over the next few years, dmus began to appear between Manchester and Rochdale and between Bradford, Halifax and Huddersfield but it was on New Years Day 1962 that the main Calder Valley service was converted to diesel operation.

A fleet of three coach trains was supplied by the Birmingham Railway Carriage & Wagon Co. Later designated class 110 or just known as 'Calder Valley' sets, their four 180 horse power engines and the ease with which they could change direction enabled them to run from Leeds to Manchester via Bradford. An hourly interval service was introduced with alternate trains running through from Harrogate to Liverpool Exchange via Wigan. These extended workings missed certain stations along the Calder Valley route until 1967-68 when through running was stopped and the service became hourly all stations from Leeds to Manchester.

A dmu service operated in the lower Calder Valley between Sowerby Bridge and York from 1962 until withdrawal at the beginning of 1970.

Station closures

Delivery of the class 110 units to the Calder Valley, marked the end of the dmu programme which had begun with the 'Derby Lightweights' in 1954. By 1962 BR were no longer singing the praises of this new type of local train service but were publishing maps implying that most of the railway mileage, including the modernised diesel routes carried only a small fraction of the traffic and that closure of over half the network was required to restore British Railways to profitability. This was the central theme of the Beeching Report which was published in 1963 and substantially implemented in the years which followed.

The main Calder Valley service was not threatened but most of its remaining branch lines were closed together with some intermediate stations.

Halifax Station entrance, about 1910.

(Peter E. Baughan collection)

Individual stations had been disappearing for some time. Copley was closed in 1931 whilst Eastwood, Cooper Bridge and three intermediate stations between Bradford and Halifax closed in the early 1950s. At some of these revenue was probably hardly enough to finance a waiting room fire but each one was fully staffed until closure with at the very least, a railman to attend the arrival and departure of every train if not a separate booking clerk and a Station Master to oversee the whole operation. Then to save costs some stations were closed in the evening and all day Sunday even though trains were running.

As closures became more serious, BR refused even to discuss ways of reducing cost as an alternative. In the period 1960-62, Smithy Bridge, Walsden, Luddendenfoot, Greetland, Elland, Thornhill and Horbury Millfield Road all shut their doors. When Smithy Bridge reopened 25 years later it was without staff but with car parking – a facility to encourage traffic which was rejected out of hand at the time of closure.

Post Beeching closures effected Low Moor and Lightcliffe in 1965 when the Bradford-Huddersfield service was withdrawn. The next year saw Newton Heath, Middleton Junction, Laisterdyke, Bramley and Armley Moor close whilst Stanningley followed at the end of 1967.

Withdrawal of the Sowerby Bridge to York trains in 1970 left the route through Brighouse without any regular passenger service and the station there was closed. Between Mirfield and Wakefield there remained a service from Huddersfield which had been expanded in the 1960s to connect with main line trains at Wakefield Westgate but none of these trains stopped at Horbury & Ossett which thus closed in 1970.

Present day passengers services

Northern Spirit run the twice hourly train from Manchester Victoria to Leeds. With departures at 23 and 48 minutes past, the service is not strictly half hourly. For much of the day, the trains are non stop from Manchester to Rochdale and alternate ones miss Walsden. Otherwise they stop at all stations. Most continue beyond Leeds to York or Selby. Evening and Sunday trains run hourly.

The hourly 'Trans Pennine Express' from Blackpool North to York or Scarborough joins the Calder Valley route at Hall Royd Junction and runs semi fast stopping at Hebden Bridge, Halifax, Bradford, New Pudsey and Leeds.

The fourth service per hour between Halifax and Leeds is formed by the train from Huddersfield and Brighouse. There is one rush hour train at 7.59 from Hebden Bridge to Leeds all stations via Brighouse and Mirfield returning at 17.12 from Leeds.

First North Western have two local trains per hour between Manchester Victoria and Rochdale but with no evening or Sunday service. These trains don't terminate at Rochdale but continue back to Manchester via Oldham. First North Western also operate two morning peak trains from Todmorden to Manchester with one early evening working in the reverse direction.

Two stretches of the original Manchester & Leeds Railway are covered by the First North Western service which run hourly, but not Sundays, from Manchester Victoria to Wakefield Westgate. At Miles Platting, this train takes the Stalybridge branch, calling at Ashton Under Lyne. It then uses the ex LNWR Standedge route before re-joining the Calder Valley line at Heaton Lodge Junction. It stops at Mirfield and leaves the M&L route when it reverses direction at

Fowler 2-6-4T No. 42408 on a Penistone to Bradford local passes an austerity 2-8-0 on the evening pick up at Hipperholme on 30 April 1959.   *(G.W. Morrison)*

The entrance to Hipperholme Station was at road level above the platforms. It looks remarkably well preserved nine years after closure.
(Peter E Baughan)

Just south of Lightcliffe Station was the exchange siding with the private system serving Brookes Non Slip Stone works. 'Silex No. 2', is seen alongside the main line in May 1962. Built by Peckett in 1931, it was sold for scrap in 1969 after the private railway had closed.
(Martin Bairstow collection)

A class 110 'Calder Valley' set leaving Ligthcliffe for Bradford Exchange on 26 March 1963.
(Martin Bairstow collection)

45216 leaving Lightcliffe with the 5.15 pm Bradford Exchange to Liverpool Exchange on 19 June 1959. The Leeds portion also called at Lightcliffe 8 minutes later and the two amalgamated at Halifax.   *(G.W. Morrison)*

A Metro-Cammell twin set with both cars powered, calls at Lightcliffe en route from Bradford Exchange to Huddersfield in 1962.   *(Peter E. Baughan)*

The 11.06 Leeds Central to Manchester Victoria, formed of two class 110 'Calder Valley' sets, rattles through Low Moor on 30 June 1962. *(Peter E. Baughan)*

2-6-4T No. 42196 at Low Moor on 17 July 1966. The engine shed here opened in 1865, was rebuilt in 1888 and closed in October 1967. *(Ian G. Holt)*

Bowling Junction Station stood on the short level stretch at the entrance to Bowling Tunnel. Despite its name, the station was never used for interchange between the two converging routes. Trains from Leeds did not stop. *(B.C. Lane collection)*

'Black Five' 4-6-0 No. 5207 passing Coal Shoots signal box on the 1 in 50 climb out of Bradford with the 10 am to Marylebone. The leading vehicle is a through Southern Railway coach to Bournemouth Central. The date is 5 May 1937.

(G.H. Butland)

0-6-0ST No. 158 by Broomfield level crossing before it was replaced by Caledonia Street bridge in 1876.

(B.C. Lane collection)

2-6-4T No. 42055 shunting at the exit from Bradford Exchange. The new (1973) station is situated at the other side of the bridge which has been filled in. (B.C. Lane)

The entrance to Bradford Exchange with separate pairs of tracks for ex L&Y (left) and GN routes. The signal box is an LMS replacement of an earlier L&Y installation. In the background stands the large L&Y Bridge St. goods depot.

(B.C. Lane collection)

The Lancashire & Yorkshire side of Bradford Exchange on 30 August 1912. The station was shared with the GNR which used the five platforms beyond the centre pillars. Ownership was exclusively L&Y.

(National Railway Museum)

Wakefield Kirkgate.

For completeness, the eastern most stretch of the original Manchester & Leeds, between Wakefield Kirkgate and Normanton, is served by the hourly Northern Spirit train from Sheffield to Leeds via Barnsley and Castleford.

Possible further development?

The pattern of service just described is by far the most frequent that the line has ever known. But there remain opportunities for enhancement.

Manchester to Bradford takes at least 64 minutes for $40\frac{1}{4}$ miles. This may be acceptable for a local service but it does not reach the standard necessary to develop longer distance travel. The problem is the nine intermediate stops rising to 12, evenings and Sundays.

What is needed is to extend the Manchester Victoria – Rochdale locals as far as Todmorden, allowing the Bradford trains to stop only at Rochdale over that section.

There is possibly no need for trains to run through beyond Leeds. All this seems to do is reduce reliability. Halifax and Bradford would still have a through service to York courtesy of the Blackpool train. It would help, though, if Manchester–Leeds trains were to start from Salford Crescent to enhance the range of connections available.

Having established a half hourly local from Manchester to Todmorden, could it not continue to Burnley? This town of 85,000 population has three stations but no credible service to Manchester. From Burnley Central you can travel every hour changing at Blackburn but it takes more than $1\frac{1}{4}$ hours. From Manchester Road Station you can do it in 1 hour 7 minutes changing at Hebden Bridge. It is doubtful if anybody does so because in the other direction the connection is generally too tight to risk.

In the brief period between March 1961 and September 1964 there was an hourly through train from Burnley Central to Manchester Victoria via the now abandoned Accrington and Bury route. A train from Burnley Manchester Road via Todmorden, even all stations, should take no more than 50 minutes. This would involve reinstatement of the west curve from the Copy Pit line into Todmorden.

The West Yorkshire PTE wants a doubling of the Halifax–Huddersfield service to half hourly. But surely the priority should be a Halifax–Brighouse–Leeds service via Dewsbury. Leeds is the focal point of West Yorkshire. It has the most commuters in its own right plus the widest choice of connections. Peripheral train services, those not radiating from Leeds or Manchester, are much harder to justify.

The PTE proposes a station at Low Moor. The problem here is what would stop? If just the Bradford–Huddersfield, then an hourly frequency would be insufficient to be worthwhile. If the Manchester trains stopped, then this would further damage their long distance credibility.

A radical proposal, which I understand is being considered, is for a half hourly express between Manchester Victoria and Leeds via the Calder Valley and Dewsbury. This is the route which was discarded as long ago as 1854 when the Leeds, Bradford & Halifax Junction opened. There might be only three stops: Rochdale, Todmorden alternating with Hebden Bridge, and Elland. The last name would be a park and ride station aimed at capturing traffic off the M62 heading for both Leeds and Manchester.

In the longer term there are two former branch lines which could be returned to passenger use fairly easily. The distance from Castleton North Junction to Heywood is only 1 mile. The line remains serviceable but its only traffic is the occasional stock movement to the preserved East Lancashire Railway. The latter extends 12 miles from Heywood to Rawtenstall. A question is whether it would be worth running a train from Manchester Victoria direct to Heywood, maybe reversing there and going onto Castleton and Rochdale. This would have to be over and above the direct service between Manchester and Rochdale.

The line between Low Moor and Thornhill has been closed since the early 1980s and the track has been lifted. But the route remains available. The West Yorkshire PTE 'Rail Plan' includes a long term aspiration for the Spen Valley. Reopening from Low Moor to Thornhill would permit a service from Bradford to Wakefield but that would not give the Spen Valley towns (Cleckheaton, Liversedge, Heckmondwike) a direct link with Leeds. There would have to be something else – maybe a curve from Ravensthorpe (L&Y) towards Dewsbury or reinstatement between Bowling Junction and Laisterdyke, or both.

The Outlook for Freight

When passenger closures began in earnest, around 1929, the lines effected invariably remained open for goods and parcels. Rishworth, Stainland and Dewsbury Market Place are all examples. Only some 30 years later did BR begin to close wayside goods yards. Then came the Beeching Report and the closure of most small yards in favour of a coal concentration scheme. With the decline of domestic coal, this system did not last long. Nor did the big marshalling yards like Healey Mills which opened in 1963, never to realise its potential.

By 1980, nearly all public goods depots had gone. One of the last to close was Halifax in December 1980. There is no freight at all now between Sowerby Bridge and Bradford and only a very occasional load of scrap between Bradford and Leeds, from a siding at Laisterdyke.

1981 saw the end of the parcels collection and delivery service. Until then, the Railway had operated a nationwide service partly duplicating that of the Post Office. The railway delivery vans, once a very familiar sight, were successors to the 'mechanical horses' which had themselves replaced actual horses. All that remains is the occasional 'red star' parcel – a premium service which sometimes uses space on passenger trains.

With the continued decline of heavy industry, modern rail freight comprises just a few specialised flows of traffic between private sidings. Stuart Carmichael keeps a record of traffic passing Littleborough. Regular flows include coal from Gascoign Wood, near Selby to Fidlers Ferry power station near Warrington. Coal for Ireland is carried in containers which are loaded onto ships at Seaforth, near Liverpool. Bitumen is carried in bogie tankers from Ellesmere Port to South Humberside. Oil coke goes from Holyhead to South Humberside whilst propylene is transported the other way from Humberside to Stanlow. There is a traffic in steel from Teesside to South Wales.

There is also some 'internal' freight including steel going to the rail welding depot at Castleton which then re-emerges as track.

Motive power is provided roughly half by former BR class 56 locos and half by the new class 66 engines ordered from General Motors by English, Welsh & Scottish Railway since privatisation.

Bradford Exchange was owned by the L&Y but platforms 6 to 10 were normally used by the Great Northern. 44693 has the 'South Yorkshireman' for Marylebone whilst through coaches to Kings Cross.
(J.C.W. Halliday)

Sometimes, L&Y and GN departures were simultaneous. 44694 is on the 8.20 to Bridlington via Halifax.
44662 has the 8.20 to Skegness via Wakefield on 26 August 1967. *(Peter Fitton)*

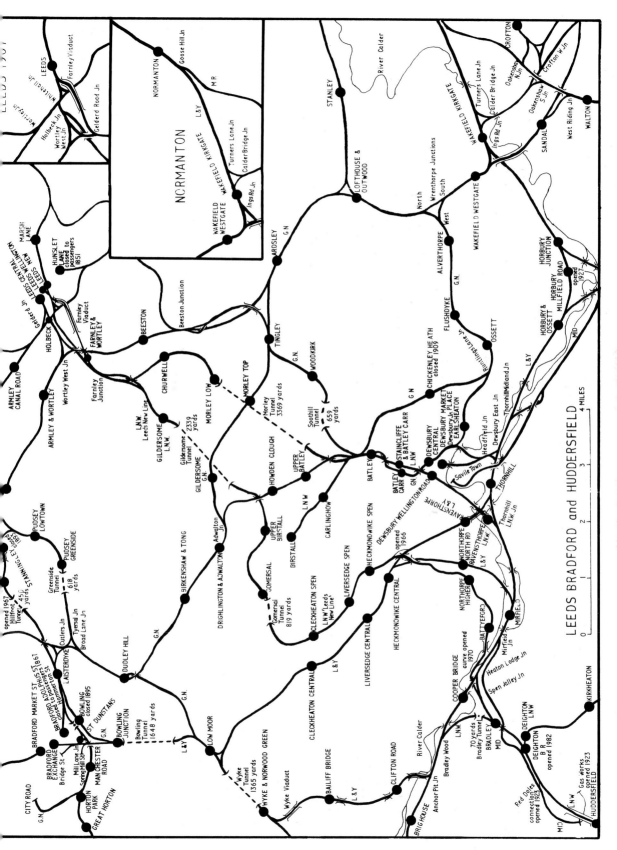

LEEDS BRADFORD and HUDDERSFIELD

NORMANTON

The 9.03 Leeds Central to Manchester Victoria approaching Bowling Junction on 17 September 1961. *(P B Booth/N E Stead collection)*

The main buildings on the Leeds bound platform at Bramley in 1965. *(John Bateman)*

Armley Moor (formerly Armley & Wortley) looking towards Bradford in 1963. *(John Bateman)*

An interior view of Leeds
Central in 1966.
(John Bateman)

Black five No. 44767, now
preserved and named 'George
Stephenson', awaiting departure
from Leeds Central. *(B.C. Lane)*

The entrance to Leeds Central
Station used by Lancashire &
Yorkshire Railway passengers.
(John Bateman)

49

Schoolboy Train Watcher and Aspiring Signalman

Tony Ross was a regular observer at Dewsbury West Junction at the end of the 1940s

Our house was about ¼ mile north of the point where Headfield Road bridged the former L&Y four-track main line south some 7 miles west of Wakefield. The bridge was almost above Dewsbury West Junction. Reading from the north, the four tracks were designated down slow, up slow, down fast, up fast. From my bedroom window I had a long-range view south eastwards across the Calder valley, over the ridged roof of the ex-L&Y Dewsbury Junction Carriage & Wagon Works. Beyond was a forest of semaphore signals on the main line around Thornhill Midland Junction.

The Carriage & Wagon Works were accessed only via Headfield Junction, on the short L&Y Dewsbury Market Place branch. This made a triangular connection northwards off the slow lines at Dewsbury East and West Junctions, the apex being Headfield Junction. My first unofficial signalbox visits were to this 45-lever box in 1949 when I was 12 years old. It was a tall brick-based structure built by the Railway Signal Company (RSC) for the L&Y in 1887 to cater for the junction with a new spur constructed by the Great Northern Railway from their Bradford-Dewsbury-Wakefield route.

The L&Y Dewsbury branch had lost its passenger service in 1930 and the GN connection had also long gone, taken out in 1933. By 1949, the box was just involved with shunting operations into and out of the Wagon Works, a couple of shunting calls per day at the adjacent chemical and gas works, and three or four pick-up trips to and from Market Place goods depot. Just the sort of place for a youngster to learn the basics of railway signalling, unhindered by passenger trains! Headfield Junction signalbox was destroyed by fire on the night of 24 October, 1949. A 7 lever ground frame replaced it. I was most upset.

I watched the much more frequent trains and signalling operations on the main line from the top of the cutting on the south side of Dewsbury West Junction. Here the sharply curved connection to Headfield Junction diverged northwards from the slow lines. The box was situated in the fork of the junction. It was a small brick-based structure built for the L&Y in 1880 by the Gloucester Wagon Company (GWC). Curiously, a 12-lever frame from an earlier box

supplied by Stevens & Sons at this location was fitted into the 1880 box. This was extended later to 24 levers to cope with quadrupling of the main line in the early 1900s. But the structure of the box itself was not extended. The larger frame was a very tight fit. There was hardly room to turn round, as I discovered when finally invited in. It was rated Class 2 and open continuously except on Sundays. It was the same class as some much larger and seemingly busier boxes that were grouped on the local omnibus telephone circuit covering a distance of about 3½ miles. East to west these were Horbury & Ossett, Healey Mills East, Healey Mills West, Thornhill Midland Junction, Dewsbury East Junction, Dewsbury West Junction, Thornhill No. 3, No. 2 and No.1.

Because block sections were short, junctions many, and traffic heavy, the descriptions of trains and their destinations were sent by verbal messages on the telephone circuit as the trains approached or passed the boxes at the circuit ends. The L&Y standard 2 pause 1 ring on the circuit phone heralded such messages announced by the signalman at the circuit end or, if he had one, by his booking boy ('train booker' in L&Y parlance). Hearing this distinctive call, the signalmen would all pick up their phones.

Individual signalmen would then take action to ensure, as far as possible, that the correct route could be set and cleared without delay. Sometimes they would agree along which line, fast or slow, the train would run. Trains joining or leaving the main line at junctions within the circuit had other distinctive call codes. Freight approaching Thornhill No. 1 bound for the old Healey Mills yard was circuit called to Healey Mills West by 2 pause 3 rings. Trains going on to or coming off the Midland branch were called by Thornhill No. 1 or Midland Junction by 3 pause 2. In passenger days on the Market Place branch, the circuit call 2 pause 2 was used between Thornhill No. 1 and Dewsbury West Junction (and vice versa), and 3 pause 1 between Dewsbury East Junction and Horbury & Ossett. Signalmen could ignore circuit calls with which they were not concerned. The circuit calls were clearly different from individual box codes that comprised

An ex L&Y 2-4-2T arrives at Headfield Junction in 1954 with two coaches for Dewsbury Carriage and Wagon Works, to the right of the fan of sidings. Just visible behind the train is Dewsbury East Junction box.
(A.M. Ross)

44692 passing Dewsbury West Junction with the 11.25 summer Saturday Scarborough Londesborough Road to Liverpool Exchange. The train is approaching Thornhill, its first scheduled stop since Bridlington apart from changing engines at Gascoigne Wood. It has averaged only 30 mph. the first carriage is an LMS/BR 'Porthole' composite in red and cream livery. *(K. Field)*

42646 passing Dewsbury East Junction, possibly with the 2.15pm (Saturdays only) Wakefield Kirkgate to Manchester Victoria about 1954. The L&Y lower quadrant signal to the right of the train is West Junctions down fast starter. East Junction only signalled the slow lines. The splitting distant is for the Royston route at Thornhill Midland Junction. *(K. Field)*

various combinations of short and long rings.

The staple main line traffic was heavy freight, with many daytime coal trains heading west and the empties coming back. Hauling most of them were Fowler 0-8-0s, and Stanier and WD 2-8-0s. Shorter trip workings had Aspinall and Fowler 0-6-0s. The top weekday passenger working was the morning refreshment car express from Liverpool Exchange to Newcastle and evening return usually in the charge of a 'Jubilee' or 'Black 5'. Aspinall 2-4-2 radial tank engines still worked some of the short Huddersfield-Wakefield Westgate express turns.

Sometimes after dark I would go just to catch something of what master railway photographer Eric Treacy described as "The Spell of the Railway". It was the firebox glow caught on the billowing steam of the frequent clanking procession of plodding freight locomotives, the steady tramp of four-wheeled wagons over the rail joins, the squeak of loose couplings and the occasional clatter of unsecured wagon brake gear levers. It was the winking and gleaming of the signal lights. It was the light over the train register desk shining through the levers and signalbox windows. It was the distinctive tones of the block bells and the shrill sounds of the circuit and control telephones which somehow seemed more audible at night. It was the thud of levers and the squeak of signal wires in the lineside pulleys.

To the east, also in the fork of its junction, was the Dewsbury East Junction box, 376 yards away. Then came Thornhill Midland Junction, 1,012 yards distant. Dewsbury East worked only the slow lines. To the west, Thornhill No. 3 was 424 yards away at the east of Thornhill station, an island platform served only by the slow lines. No. 3 worked the slow lines and the east end bay platform, once used by the shuttle passenger service to Dewsbury Market Place. Thornhill No. 2 was 844 yards away at the west end of the station. It worked all four lines, running crossovers, and a bay platform. Thornhill No.1 box was 1,280 yards away, within the fork of the junction between the slow lines and the branch to Heckmondwike. No. 1 also controlled sidings on both sides of the main line and branch. On the Dewsbury branch to the north, Headfield Junction was 435 yards away from West Junction, around the sharply curved connection. In 1949 Dewsbury East Junction and Thornhill No. 3 were single shift weekday boxes, switched out at other times.

The five block instruments on the shelf above Dewsbury West Junction's lever frame were traditional L&Y. The bell signals were sent using a plunger in the centre of the instrument commutator that was operated by the palm of the hand. There was a knack to this that I never quite mastered as a 12 or 13-year-old; bell tappers were much easier to use.

Originally only two (Nos. 7 and 11) of the 24 levers in Dewsbury West Junction were spare, and no less than 11 of them operated distant signals! Because of the short block sections, two and sometimes even three distants (slotted with the starting and/or home signals of the boxes in the rear) were required to give acceptable braking distances. After the Dewsbury branch passenger service was withdrawn, the two down slow to down branch splitting inner distants (Nos. 18 and 19) were removed, and the up branch distant (No. 12) was taken out of use.

But even two or three distants did not always provide the necessary braking distance at line speed. So a system known as 'distant signal indicator working' was used at Thornhill No. 2 and Dewsbury West Junction. At the latter, the up main distants (No. 1 on the fast, and

Nos. 8 and 9 on the slow) were led by the Thornhill No. 2 up distants (which were in turn led by the Thornhill No. 1 up distants). Two wire-operated, mechanical slide-type indicators behind the frame showed when Thornhill No. 2's up fast or up slow distants had been pulled off. Only then was the West Junction man permitted to pull off his own up fast or up slow distants. The slides were quiet in operation and the 'off' display of No. 2's distants could sometimes be missed. You may ask how did Thornhill No. 3 fit into this system? Well, No. 3's up slow 'distant' was just a slot on No. 2's up slow outer distant, below West Junction's up slow (and up branch) home.

On the down slow, West Junction's three distants (Nos. 22, 23 and 24) could not be cleared until Dewsbury East Junction's outer distant had been pulled off. This was never missed as it was signalled by the violent rotation of a wire-operated indicator disc located somewhere near the train register desk. It rattled the whole box.

We moved from Dewsbury to Bridlington during Easter 1951. Grandparents lived in Ossett so I was still able to visit my former railway haunts during school holidays. University and a career in chemical engineering beckoned and youthful railway signalling ambitions were sidelined. Dewsbury West Junction closed on 29 May, 1960. Access to the branch thereafter was via Dewsbury East Junction. Today the 'branch' provides access only to the cement terminal on the site of the Wagon Works, closed in June 1967. The main line was 'dequadrified' in 1985. Thornhill Nos. 2 and 3 boxes were early closures in 1958. The functions of the other neighbouring signalboxes were transferred to the new Healey Mills power box on 16 June, 1963.

The lever frame and block shelf at Dewsbury West Junction, shortly before closure of the box in 1960.
(A.M. Ross)

52

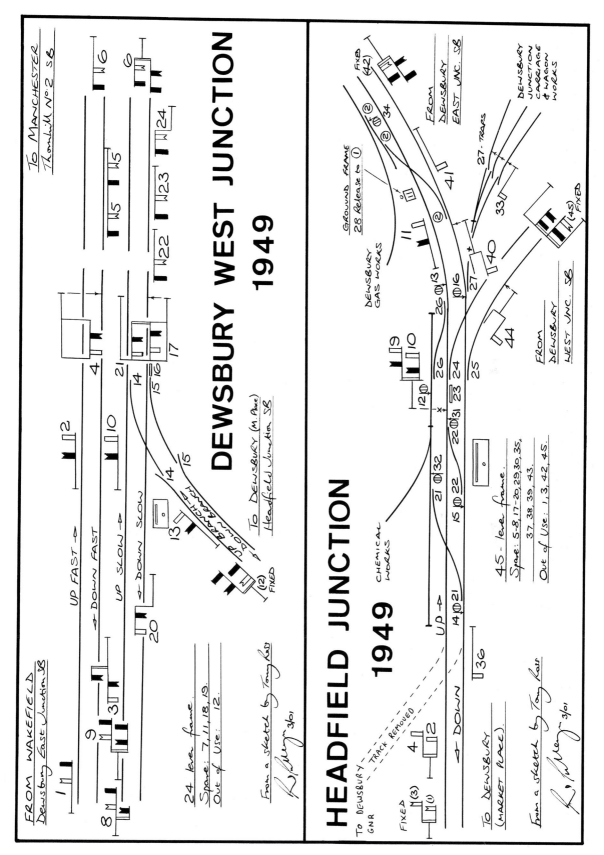

DEWSBURY WEST JUNCTION
1949

TO MANCHESTER
Thornhill No 2 SB

FROM WAKEFIELD
Dewsbury East Junction SB

UP FAST →
← DOWN FAST
UP SLOW →
← DOWN SLOW

UP BRANCH →
& DOWN BRANCH

TO DEWSBURY (M. Place)
Headfield Junction SB

24 lever frame.
Spare: 7,11,18,19.
Out of Use: 12.

From a sketch by Tony Ross

HEADFIELD JUNCTION
1949

GROUND FRAME
28 Release to ①

FROM
DEWSBURY
EAST JNC. SB

DEWSBURY
JUNCTION
CARRIAGE
& WAGON
WORKS

27. TRAPS

FROM
DEWSBURY
WEST JNC. SB

DEWSBURY
GAS WORKS

45 - lever frame.
Spare: 5-8,17-20,29,30,35,
37,38,39,43.
Out of Use: 1,3,42,45.

CHEMICAL
WORKS

TO DEWSBURY
GNR
TRACK REMOVED

FIXED

← DOWN

UP →

TO DEWSBURY
(MARKET PLACE)

From a sketch by Tony Ross

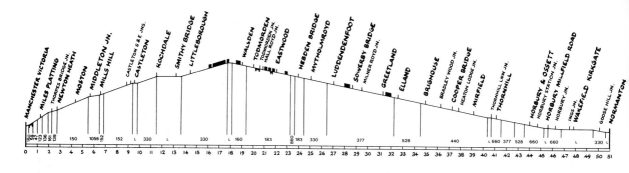

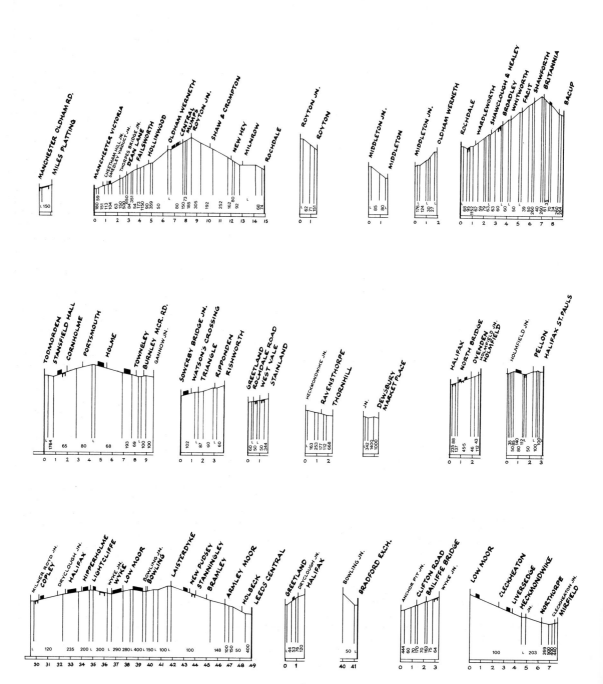

The Copy Pit route

Hall Royd Junction on 30 March 1964. A relief service to Blackpool takes the Copy Pit route in the charge of 'Jubilee' 4-6-0 No. 45694 'Bellerophon'.
(Ian G. Holt)

An important adjunct to the Calder Valley Line is the heavily engineered and steeply graded branch into Lancashire which after a period of neglect has recently come back into prominence.

In 1845 the Manchester & Leeds Railway was authorised to build a branch from Todmorden through the Cliviger Gorge to Burnley. Work was suspended during the winter of 1847/48 in the post Railway Mania crisis but was resumed and a single track opened to Burnley Thorneybank on 12 November 1849 following a Board of Trade inspection on 27 October and the running of a Director's special three days later.

The following year saw a short extension opened to Gannow Junction, near Rose Grove where the Todmorden line joined the East Lancashire Railway's Colne to Preston route. This created a Trans-Pennine railway between West Yorkshire, East Lancashire and the Fylde Coast. To avoid reversal at Todmorden a curve was provided in 1862 between Hall Royd Junction and Stansfield Hall but, so that Yorkshire to Blackpool trains did not forget Todmorden altogether, a station called Stansfield Hall for Todmorden was opened in 1869 on the outskirts of the town. The track had been doubled throughout in 1860. Burnley Thorneybank Station was replaced by nearby Manchester Road in 1866.

'Bradshaw' for 1910 shows 14 local trains from Todmorden to Rose Grove fairly evenly spaced between 8.03 am and 10.30 pm. None of them stopped at Stansfield Hall but otherwise most called at every station and most ran through at least as far as Accrington. As was customary on most lines, there was an extra late train on a Saturday at 11.40 from Todmorden to Burnley Manchester Road which called

at Cornholme and Portsmouth. There were five local trains on a Sunday.

The morning Halifax to Blackpool train called at Stansfield Hall at 9.17 also serving Towneley, Burnley Manchester Road and Rose Grove. On Mondays, it was preceeded by a Bradford to Blackpool service which called at Stansfield Hall at 8.33. The next 'express' was a through train from Wakefield Kirkgate to Blackburn which ran via Thornhill, Cleckheaton and Halifax reaching Stansfield Hall at 3.19 pm. Another Wakefield to Blackburn service hit Stansfield Hall at 8.22 pm. This travelled via Brighouse and conveyed a through carriage which had left Kings Cross at 3.25pm.

There were no 'express' services over the Copy Pit route on a Sunday in Winter. There were however additional excursion and relief trains from various Yorkshire towns to Blackpool in Summer especially at Bank Holidays.

Intermediate passenger traffic was light and station closures began with Holme in 1930. By 1961 they had all disappeared from the timetable the last to go being Burnley Manchester Road. A non stop 'local' service continued between Todmorden and Rose Grove until 1965. The long standing Leeds to Blackpool train continued each morning but in Summer only after 1976.

It was for freight that the Copy Pit route was resignalled and brought under the control of Preston power box in the early 1970s. By this time, traffic had disappeared from the Todmorden to Stansfield Hall curve which was officially closed in March 1973. After the 1965 passenger closure, there had still been a Brewery Sidings to Rose Grove freight and there were light engine movements to Rose Grove shed until the end of steam on BR in August 1968.

'Standard' 4-6-0s Nos 73134 and 73069 head a special across Lydgate Viaduct on the climb from Todmorden towards Copy Pit Summit on 20 April 1968. *(Ian G. Holt)*

Black Five No. 44988 passing Copy Pit box with a Blackpool about 1960. *(Martin Bairstow collection)*

The volume of freight declined and, by the early 1980s, the daily Immingham to Preston oil train was the only booked working over Copy Pit. When this was diverted, the route saw no trains at all on most days through the winter. Complete closure was threatened in the 'Corporate Plan' published by BR in 1983.

Then came a change of heart with BR apparently seeing some potential in a route connecting the conurbations of West Yorkshire and East Lancashire. October 1984 saw the launch of six trains each weekday between Leeds and Preston with some workings extended to Blackpool. Initially trains called at Rose Grove as the nearest point to Burnley but a rebuilt Manchester Road Station opened in October 1986.

The service was later increased to hourly and since 1994 has formed part of the 'Trans Pennine Express' network. It runs semi fast from York to Blackpool North, through from Scarborough on alternate hours. It does not consistently live up to the standard of other 'Trans Pennine' routes. Refurbished class 158 units appear on only some workings and refreshment trolleys are rarely seen.

The route described

The Leeds to Blackpool train is brought almost to a stand between Castle Hill and Millwood Tunnels because of the approach control at Hall Royd Junction where the permitted speed for the Burnley line is much lower than for trains going to Manchester. Once over the junction, the train negotiates a series of reverse curves and begins the 1 in 65 ascent. Kitson Wood, the first of three tunnels leads directly onto Lydgate Viaduct after which the line continues to twist along a ledge on the hillside until the valley begins to widen beyond Portsmouth. The gradient eases to 1 in 80 for the last mile and a half to Copy Pit summit where the line begins to fall at 1 in 68.

The effect of the 1986 landslip which closed the route from February until October, can be seen at the entrance to Holme Tunnel which has been reinforced for the first few yards hopefully to prevent further trouble. The descent continues through wooded country but emerging from Towneley Tunnel the town of Burnley comes into view. The signal box at Towneley Station protects the level crossing but is not a block post as the line is controlled from Preston.

Burnley Manchester Road stands on the same site as the earlier station and is on the edge of the town which is also served by two stations on the Colne line which we join at Gannow Junction. Trains from Leeds no longer stop at Rose Grove which is now just a bare island platform. The sidings and engine sheds have been completely removed from what was once an important junction.

The Problem of Overcrowding

A problem with the Leeds-Blackpool service is the seasonal imbalance in the load. Travel in Winter, or even on most weekdays in Summer and you can have room to spare. Risk a peak time journey on a Summer Saturday and you may have to endure two hours of serious discomfort.

I am writing this paragraph at Hebden Bridge having just come from New Pudsey by the 9.27 Blackpool train on a July Saturday. I managed to get a seat, first by occupying one reserved from Bradford and then switching before the Bradford crowd got on. I have the advantage of travelling with only a light shoulder bag. Many people had heavy luggage. We left Bradford with passengers sitting on the luggage racks. It may get worse after Burnley.

The train was a three coach class 158 with 2½ coaches over subscribed and an empty first class section occupying the remaining half carriage. It is possible that this demarcation will be overwhelmed before the train leaves Preston.

There is no easy answer. We can't go back to the pre Beeching practice of maintaining resources just for seasonal peaks. The fare structure already encourages off peak travel. As suggested in a later chapter, the first class section should be declassification on this route. This was a three coach train. Most are only two. Extra carriages do not exist. If/when they become available, it should be possible to strengthen trains such as this one on Saturdays at the expense of commuter trains which need strengthening only on Mondays to Fridays. This requires complicated (and intensive) rostering of rolling stock and there will still be times when things fail to go according to plan. The strengthening set is always the one they borrow to relieve problems elsewhere.

8F No. 48410 takes the Copy Pit route at Hall Royd Junction on 18 May 1968. Sister engine 48419 is the Copy Pit banker standing on south to west curve in the background.
(Martin Bairstow collection)

The 13.40 Blackpool South to Bradford dmu rounds the curve above Towneley on 16 July 1966. *(Ian G. Holt)*

WD 2-8-0 No. 90249 banking a coal train towards Copy Pit Summit on 14 October 1961. The train engine is No. 90557. *(Martin Bairstow collection)*

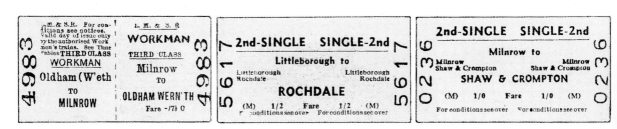

Jubilee 4-6-0 No. 45565 'Victoria' passing Portsmouth Ground Frame box on 23 July 1966 with a Leeds to Blackpool working.   *(Ian G. Holt)*

A twin powered Cravens set on the Todmorden to Rose Grove service above Portsmouth on 30 September 1961.
            (Ian G. Holt)

Freight engines were pressed into service on extra workings to Blackpool. 4F 0-6-0 No. 44233 passing Copy Pit Summit returning towards Halifax in 1957.

(Martin Bairstow collection)

Bucket and Spade Traffic

'Britannia' class No. 70039 Sir Christopher Wren entering Sowerby Bridge with a Cleethorpes to Blackpool working in September 1963. *(Peter Sunderland)*

A familiar sight, until the mid 1960s, were the rakes of coaches strewn around wayside sidings. These stood idle for much of the year but were called into service for holiday and excursion traffic.

In August 1950, the Chairman of British Railways confirmed 'the continuation of excursion trips for those of modest means'. This sounds a bit patronising because you didn't need to be poor to travel on an excursion. The fares were cheaper than normal on the principle that the trains were better filled if you could harness groups of people all travelling to the same popular destinations.

Each Thursday during that summer, the *Halifax Courier* carried an advertisement of forthcoming excursions. Generally it just gave the departure time and the fare from Halifax and other local stations. In addition it devoted editorial space to report how business was doing and to offer related anecdotes.

On 4 July 1950, the paper commented that few excursions now left before 8am. It recalled that, before the First World War, excursionists could regularly be seen taking a brisk walk to the station before 6am so they could be strolling on the prom by 9 o'clock. But that generation had been accustomed to early hours at the factories and mills.

The local press would send a reporter to see how bookings were going at certain stations. On the eve of Halifax Wakes Week, the *Courier* reported that Blackpool had lost some of its former popularity with more tickets being sold to Bridlington and Scarborough than to West Coast resorts. This assertion was on the basis of advanced bookings at Sowerby Bridge and Luddendenfoot.

At the former station, the staff were expecting another prize in the station gardens competition. The area between the up platform and the Rishworth branch had a good lay out. It was tidy and colourful with really attractive flowerbeds. When the station came to be judged, the general appearance and cleanliness of the station premises would be taken into account but, fortunately, allowance would be made for the fact that the buildings and canopies were in a 'shocking condition'.

The *Courier* reported that again no excursions would be offered from the Rishworth branch. It recalled that special trains had continued after the passenger closure in 1929 but there had been nothing since the outbreak of War in 1939.

For an insight into real 'classic' excursions, the reporter had turned to Thomas Normington for inspiration. In 1848, an excursion was offered from Oldham to Blackpool at one shilling for women but one shilling and sixpence for men. According to Normington, the Superintendent of the line suspected that a lot of men were cheating by turning up dressed in female attire. He deputed an assistant to stand on a chair holding up a long pole with a notice that ladies were to board the train first, allowing the

D7609 passing Eastwood with a Blackpool excursion on 20 August 1966. *(Ian G. Holt)*

'Crab' 2-6-0 No. 42783 stands in the up main platform at Rochdale with a Bradford Exchange to Llandudno train on 28 July 1962. Sister engine No. 42702 has a Wigan local ready to leave from one of the up bays.

(Ian G. Holt)

'Jubilee' class No. 45593 'Kolhapur' entering Halifax with a Bradford to Blackpool extra on 28 March 1967.
(Martin Bairstow collection)

Superintendent to satisfy himself as to their authenticity. Couples refused to separate and the Superintendent was knocked over in the resultant stampede. By the time he came round, the train was on its way.

In 1858, the Sowerby Bridge Temperance Society held their annual trip to Liverpool. When they returned in the small hours of the morning, four truck loads of drunken passengers had to be wheeled off the platform into the station yard whence their friends got them home as best they could.

The second week in July was Halifax Wakes Week. 22 additional trains were scheduled to leave Halifax Old Station on Friday evening/Saturday morning 7/8 July 1950. According to the *Courier*, Blackpool was not so well favoured as in previous years but there were good bookings to Scarborough, North Wales, Cleethorpes and Yarmouth. From Sunday 9 to Friday 14, day excursion tickets were offered by ordinary train from local stations to any station with a 60 mile radius. Throughout the week, there was a programme of special excursion trains. On Monday 10, the *Courier* reported that day excursions to Blackpool had been well filled but then there had been a lull until midday for half day fares to apply.

There was a steady flow of westbound excursion trains from mid morning:

Wyke & NG	11.04	11.33	11.40	12.40
Lightcliffe	11.07	11.37	11.44	12.45
Hipperholme	11.10	11.41	11.48	12.50
Halifax	11.27	11.47	11.54	12.57
Greetland	-	-	-	13.03
Elland	-	-	-	13.06
Brighouse	-	-	-	13.14
Sowerby Bridge	11.35	11.55	12.02	-
Luddendenfoot	-	12.00	12.07	-
Destination	Llandudno	Liverpool	Blackpool	Belle Vue

The Llandudno trip was via Liverpool Exchange and the Liverpool & North Wales Steam Packet Company. The trip to Belle Vue, near Manchester included admission to the pleasure gardens.

Other excursions ran to the East Coast and to sporting events. On Wednesday and Thursday 12 and 13 July there was a special from Halifax, Greetland, Elland and Brighouse to Pontefract Tanshelf for the Races.

On Wednesday 13 July, a party of 25 school children left Halifax Station at 10pm for a fortnight in Aachen. They had originally intended to leave earlier and stay overnight in an air raid shelter in Clapham, South London. But that facility had been commandeered for troops driving lorries during a strike at Smithfield Market.

The *Rochdale Observer* carried similar advertisements for day excursions. Here, the emphasis was on West Coast destinations, principally Blackpool and Southport. There were full day, half day and evening trips at differential fares, the later you set out, the less it cost. Some Blackpool trips offered reduced price admission to the Tower or Winter Gardens. There were excursions to Liverpool with through bookings to New Brighton either by ferry or by the Mersey Railway. Llandudno could be reached either by train all the way or by steamer from Liverpool.

On Sunday 18 June 1950, a trip was offered to Lancaster and stations to Barrow in Furness changing at Bolton. On the same day, there was a through excursion to Scarborough Londesborough Road

The platform indicator at Rochdale announcing a departure for North Wales, 1962. *(R.S. Greenwood)*

picking up at Castleton and Rochdale. For people who didn't want to go that far, they advertised an excursion to Sowerby Bridge, Halifax and Bradford Exchange at 11.25am from Rochdale, returning at 7.30pm from Bradford.

They even took newspaper space to advertise trips from Rochdale to Milnrow for a cricket match at a return fare of 5d on Saturday 10 June. On 12 and 13 July, Rochdale 'punters' were offered excursion tickets to Pontefract Races but they had to change at Wakefield Kirkgate.

Publicly advertised excursions were supplemented with trains chartered by Sunday schools, working mens clubs and other organisations. In these instances, the organisers paid a fee for the train and sold tickets at their own profit or loss. The tickets themselves were conventional Edmondson cards issued by the Railway Company.

The whole industry of special, excursion and even Saturday holiday trains went into rapid decline in the mid 1960s. The Beeching Report was particularly critical of rolling stock held in reserve for seasonal or occasional use. Today the ordinary trains are more frequent, running to the same timetable all year round. There are no resources to relieve Summer peaks, still less to encourage them.

Jubilee class 4-6-0 No. 45719 'Glorious' storms through Smithy Bridge with Rugby League special from Wigan to Wakefield on 24 March 1962.

(R.S. Greenwood)

90337 entering Littleborough with a Todmorden to Southport excursion on 20 May 1961. *(Ian G. Holt)*

Return to Brighouse

150273 working the 17.15 Bradford to Huddersfield deposits a few passengers at Brighouse on 1 June 2000.
(Martin Bairstow collection)

In the context of more than 160 years history, the reopening of Brighouse should merit no more than a paragraph rather than a chapter. Yet I give it this coverage to demonstrate just how hard it is to restore a facility, however modest.

All it involved was the reintroduction of regular passenger trains over less than ten route miles previously carrying freight and occasional passenger traffic. Two unstaffed stations were to be provided but one of them proved too difficult. The idea had been talked about ever since the West Yorkshire PTE was formed in 1974. It had been official policy since at least 1986. The two disused curves and attendant signalling were still open when the scheme was first proposed.

Each time the project was delayed, the price rose – and not just with inflation. In the run up to privatisation, all the different 'profit centres' had to establish their right to a 'cut'. They all had to pour scorn on previous 'inadequate' BR costings.

On 16 November 1993, the *Halifax Courier* carried an article headed 'Action Stations' with an editorial comment that, at £2 million, the scheme was a bargain. Six years later the cost had trebbled. Railtrack decided that the two disused sections had to be rebuilt completely and that a bridge carrying heavy freight trains was insufficient to support a dmu.

The specifications for the stations grew from the wooden halts of the 1980s, like Bramley and Walsden, to a point where Elland had to be dropped because even the swollen budget could not accommodate new requirements such as easier gradients on pedestrian ramps.

Capital costs were underwritten by 'City Challenge' funding from the Government. These were announced in 1994 but there was no corresponding support for running costs which also multiplied with privatisation. In 1997 the PTE decided to press ahead without revenue support for fear of losing the capital funding. As work finally got underway in the Autumn of 1999, it was announced that the budget would cover only one station so Brighouse was built and Elland abandoned.

Finally the service opened on Sunday 29 May 2000 with an hourly train (2 hourly on Sundays) between Leeds, Bradford, Halifax and Huddersfield. This already ran as far as Halifax except that it now stands longer in Bradford. It then stands six minutes in Halifax giving a 45 minute journey from Bradford to Huddersfield. It only took 31 minutes with the same two stops prior to closure in 1965. The distance is 18 miles by rail but only 12 by road.

Brighouse to Leeds via Bradford takes 55 minutes – for 23 miles by rail, but only 16 by road. This journey can be done by motorway. One direct train is provided in the morning peak at 8.10 from Brighouse returning at 17.12 from Leeds, all stations via Dewsbury.

Historically, Brighouse had trains to Huddersfield, Bradford, Wakefield and Manchester but never to Leeds except in the short period 1848-1854.

At Huddersfield, I joined the second train on the first day. I was pleased to see two passengers with airline luggage alight from Manchester Airport and change straight onto the adjacent train for Brighouse. I was much less impressed three days later when I tried to catch the 17.48 from Brighouse to New Pudsey. With a *Halifax Courier* reporter present to record the first rush hour (after the bank holiday), they managed to cancel the train and failed to use the public address system, leaving press and public stranded for an hour with neither train nor information.

For traffic to grow, as it has at other stations, the trains need to be fast, frequent and reliable. So far Brighouse seems to have failed all three tests. One can only hope that this is just the beginning of something more substantial.

No Return to Elland

Rod Bailey, Commercial Manager of the Middleton Railway, also has doubts about the revived Halifax–Huddersfield. His grievance is the failure to reopen Elland Station. Rod has some authority to speak for the commuters of Elland. From September 1957, he travelled by rail to Bradford Grammar

School. It was not a simple journey.

He could leave Elland at the early hour of 7.23 arriving at Bradford Exchange at 8.00. He must have done this occasionally because then he was able to catch the 8.23 or 8.30 from Forster Square Station to Frizinghall.

More usually, he caught the 8.03 from Elland, a Normanton to Halifax working which ran to serve the parcels distribution system as much as the travelling public. At Halifax there was a wait until 8.26 for a Manchester to Leeds train which was doubled headed – a pair of 'Black Fives' or sometimes a 'Patriot' or 'Jubilee'. This reached Low Moor at 8.37. On the adjacent platform, the Huddersfield to Bradford via Cleckheaton was already waiting. Usually a Fowler tank with three coaches, it stood at Low Moor for five minutes so as to connect both into and out of the Manchester–Leeds train. Bradford Exchange was reached at 8.47. It was then a trolley bus to reach school about 9am. The return journey was straight

forward enough thanks to an 'early pass' which allowed Rod to leave school before the normal 4.15pm. This enabled him to catch the 4.28 from Bradford Exchange, arriving Elland at 4.57. The next train at 4.50 didn't reach Elland until 5.33 because it stood 18 minutes at Halifax.

By 1960, the diesels had brought a slightly faster and more frequent service but a number of peak hour trains remained steam hauled, not least for the volume of parcels they carried. The 7.24 dmu from Elland reached Bradford at 7.49. The 8.01 steam train still needed the two changes to reach Bradford Exchange at 8.47.

A year later, the Normanton to Halifax did not leave Elland until 8.28 making it impossible to use the train for school. Elland Station closed in September 1962.

The proposed but discarded new station was at Lowfields, 1/2 mile towards Brighouse, where an industrial estate has been developed on the site of the former power station.

Fairburn 2-6-4T No. 42084 attacking the 1 in 44 from Greetland towards Dryclough Junction with through carriages from Kings Cross to Halifax on 29 April 1962.
(Martin Bairstow collection)

A B1 and a 'Black Five' head the Newcastle to Red Bank (Manchester) empty newspaper vans through the island platform at Elland, closed in 1962.
(Peter Sunderland)

Finding the way to Elland

This is extracted from a letter sent by Mr Crosland to his wife Hannah, temporarily in Egremont looking after a relative. The 'packet' would be the Mersey Ferry. The 'two booking places' would be for the Liverpool & Manchester and for the Manchester & Leeds Companies at Victoria Station. 'Huddersfield' means Cooper Bridge Station. Unfortunately, I have misplaced the name of the gentleman who let me have a copy of his ancestor's correspondence.
Oakes Nr Huddersfield
August 27th 1845

Dear Wife,
When you return be very careful when you get on And of the packet. If you leave Liverpool at half past twelve o'clock you will get to Elland soon after six o'clock at night. If you let us know the day you are coming we can meet you at Elland with the carr. You will have to book at Liverpool For Manchester And at Manchester for Elland. Their is two booking places at Manchester. You will have to inquire for the place to book for Huddersfield but you must only book for Elland as the Fair will be less.
From your most Respectfully
Benjamin Crosland

```
2nd-SINGLE    SINGLE-2nd
        Halifax (Town) to
Halifax (Town)            Halifax (Town)
Greetland etc.               Elland etc.
      ELLAND or GREETLAND
  (N)   0/6   Fare   0/6   (N)
For conditions see over   For conditions see over
```

It was once a common practice for invoices and letterheads to include a picture of the Mill or factory premises. The train passing T&B Taylor's establishment must be travelling very fast for the smoke to go the opposite way to the prevailing wind.

Lancashire Branch Lines

Oldham and Royton

The branch to Oldham was authorised by the same Act as that to Halifax in 1839. Work commenced in July 1841 and opening was achieved on 31 March 1842. This was three days after Easter Monday for which the directors had hoped to have trains running but Lt. Col. Pasley, the Government Inspector was unavailable to visit the line until after his Easter holiday. Planned by George Stephenson and executed by Thomas Longridge Gooch, the elder brother of Daniel Gooch, later Chairman of the GWR, the branch left the main line at Middleton Station (renamed Middleton Junction in 1852) on a sharp curve which necessitated a 15 mph speed restriction. The principal feature was the rope worked Werneth incline by which trains climbed for ¾ mile at 1 in 27. It had been proposed to work this on the principle of self balancing up and down trains but the idea was rejected because of the inconvenience anticipated in always having to arrange simultaneous up and down movements when, in particular, trains from Coppice Nook pit near the summit might wish to be despatched regardless of balancing workings. Instead, all up and down trains were operated on one track and a train of ballast wagons, just dead weight, ran up and down the other line. An ascending train would stop at the foot of the incline to attach the rope. It would then set back a little to lift the ballast wagons off chocks at the summit before proceeding under the combined power of its own locomotive, the winding engine and the weight of the ballast wagons. In 1847 the branch was extended from Werneth by means of two tunnels to a station nearer the town centre at Oldham Mumps. The first Station Master here was none other than Thomas Normington who recalls travelling as a

passenger on the last train from Manchester Victoria to Oldham Mumps one evening when the rope broke and the train stopped on the Werneth incline. The driver informed him "It's all up lad, we shall have to stop here all neet". "Nonsense" retorted Normington, imploring the driver to return to the foot of the incline and try to ascend under locomotive power alone. The driver reluctantly agreed, set back, disposed of all but two coaches and a van and duly made the attempt. The train stalled after 300 yards. Normington told him that he had not tried hard enough nor raised sufficient steam. 'Some sharp words' passed between them before the train was set back even further to take a longer run at the incline. Werneth was reached at the second attempt to a 'good hearty cheer' from the passengers 'for accomplishing what was considered to be an impossibility'. If Normington's account is true the locomotive was a 2-2-2 No. 131. built in 1849. He goes on to claim that as a direct result of his action further tests were held, more powerful locomotives provided and passenger trains worked under their own power from 1851. Other sources suggest that rope working ceased in 1854.

In 1861, the London & North Western and Manchester Sheffield & Lincolnshire Railways opened the joint Oldham, Ashton & Guide Bridge line. This was described in *The Leeds, Huddersfield & Manchester Railway*. The principal station was Oldham Clegg Street which was provided with a direct service to Manchester London Road (now Piccadilly). The L&Y responded by building an adjacent station called Oldham Central. Interchange between Clegg Street and Central was easy provided passengers did not mind going outside and crossing the

Ex L&Y 2-4-2T No. 50850 assisted in the rear by 3F 0-6-0 No. 52271 attacking the 1 in 27 incline between Middleton Junction and Oldham Werneth.   *(J. Davenport)*

The 6.15 pm Rochdale to Manchester Victoria between New Hey and Shaw hauled by 'Standard' 4-6-0 No. 75046 on 4 July 1958.
(Peter Hutchinson)

The entrances to Central (left) and Clegg Street (right) confronted each other from opposite sides of the road. 1966. *(G.C. Lewthwaite)*

'Standard' 2-6-4T No. 80088 leaving Oldham Mumps with a Rochdale to Manchester Victoria train in June 1955. The coach is a remnant of the LMS 'Coronation Scot' sets.
(J. Davenport)

street. The absence of a direct link at platform level together with adoption of the name 'Central' suggests that the L&Y station was built as much to upstage the opposition as to provide a connection with the establishment next door.

The extension from Oldham Mumps to Rochdale was first authorised by an Act of 1847 but abandoned as capital was not available in the Post Railway Mania period to carry out all the new lines which had been approved. An Act of 1859 revived the scheme and the extension opened in 1863. A branch to Royton, double track and descending at 1 in 62 towards the terminus, was completed the following year.

It took rather longer to achieve the railway from Thorpes Bridge Junction to Oldham Werneth via Hollinwood which had also first been authorised in 1847. When completed in 1880, this route which climbed at 1 in 50 for half its length offered a less severe alternative to that via Middleton Junction and most Manchester to Oldham trains then took the Hollinwood route.

The Werneth incline nevertheless retained a regular passenger service until 1958. After that occasional passenger trains used it until 1960. On 5 January 1963 Class 8F 2-8-0 No 48546 hauled a brake van special to mark the final closure of the line.

Following electrification to Bury in 1916, it had been the intention of the L&Y to extend the system to Oldham but war and subsequent shortage of capital ensured that the Bury line remained the only electric service out of Manchester Victoria. Steam trains continued until the introduction of dmus on 9 June 1958. A 20 minute interval service then commenced between Manchester and Oldham continuing alternately to Rochdale and Royton. On Sundays the diesels ran hourly from Manchester to Rochdale.

The Beeching Report listed the Oldham line for 'modification'. In 1964 BR confirmed their intention to close it, withdrew the Sunday trains and cut off peak services, especially to Royton. They did not proceed with closure from Manchester to Oldham Mumps, but the Royton service ended on 16 April 1966. Oldham Central Station closed on the same date having lost much of its purpose since the demise of Clegg Street in 1959. In 1971 the Minister of Transport authorised closure between Mumps and Rochdale but the line was salvaged, initially on a short term basis, by the recently formed PTE. This support was threatened when, in 1973, the Government refused to sanction the PTE's 'Picc-Vic' scheme which was to have revitalised services to the north of Manchester by linking them with those on the south side.

From 1979, trains ran half hourly from Manchester to Shaw & Crompton then hourly to Rochdale. The track between Shaw and Rochdale was singled in 1980. All the branch stations except Oldham Mumps had been unstaffed since 1969 but Shaw & Crompton regained a ticket office in 1993.

An additional station opened at Derker in 1985 replacing the less convenient Royton Junction which retained a tiny number of stops pending closure two years later. 1985 also saw the introduction of class 142 dmus on the Oldham service. Now considered inadequate because of their four wheels and bus seats, they can at least get up the gradients better than their predecessors.

The service increased during the 1990s. The present timetable offers four departures an hour from Manchester Victoria. Alternate trains run all stations to Shaw & Crompton. The others run fast to Oldham

8F 2-8-0 No. 48546 has stalled just short of the Summit as it attempts to surmount the Werneth Incline with the last brake van special on 5 January 1963. Meanwhile the road has been reset for a dmu coming up the easier graded Hollinwood line. *(Ian G. Holt)*

Mumps then Shaw & Crompton, New Hey, Milnrow and Rochdale. This means the single track section from Shaw to Rochdale is occupied at 100% capacity for most of the day.

The only surviving freight traffic is over the ½ mile nearest Thorpes Bridge Junction. Up to 600 tonnes of domestic refuse per day can be removed from sidings opened at Dean Lane in 1981 where there is also a stone terminal. Otherwise the Oldham line is now a passenger only railway. An editorial in *Modern Railways* for January 1967 said of Oldham's parcels traffic: "The town's Clegg St. depot (then connected to the ex L&Y branch) does a thriving business with the mail order firms that have revived the fortunes of the cotton mill territory. Sound organisation both at the depot and in the mail order firms' own premises, where BR staff pre-sort the despatches, have cut the costs to a keenly competitive level per package, which virtually guarantees the traffic long term". This traffic ceased in 1981 when BR withdrew completely from its collection and delivery parcels service.

The expanse of railway owned land between Mumps Station and the entrance to Central Tunnel is now a derelict eyesore as are the remains of the line's other one-time freight facilities. The large coal yards at Royton Junction and Failsworth and the large cotton warehouses at Hartford Sidings (between Mumps and Royton Junction), at Hollinwood and at Werneth have succumbed to the decline in traditional industries and the 'streamlining' of BR freight operation.

142011 approaching New Hey with a Manchester Victoria to Rochdale working on 22 February 1986.
(Tom Heavyside)

A Rochdale to Manchester Victoria service has left Oldham Mumps and is passing Clegg Street parcels depot on 23 May 1979.
(Tom Heavyside)

80093 restarting a Manchester to Rochdale train from Oldham Central in 1957. The platform in the foreground belongs to the adjacent Clegg Street Station. *(J. Davenport)*

'Black five' 4-6-0 No. 45196 leaving Clegg Street with the evening parcels to Carnforth in July 1967. The train has crossed over from the OA&GB on to the L&Y line. *(J. Davenport)*

Greater Manchester Metrolink

Mention was made earlier of the 'Gresley Pacific' whistles now heard at Manchester Victoria as the Metrolink tram arrives from Bury and then continues its journey at street level through the City Centre.

Opened in 1992, Metrolink was the eventual substitute for the 'Picc-Vic' underground line aborted nearly 20 years earlier.

In essence, Metrolink involved converting the existing electric railways from Victoria to Bury and from Piccadilly to Altrincham and connecting them with about two miles of street tramway in the City Centre.

The effect has been threefold:

1. To bridge the historic gap in the railway network between north and south Manchester.
2. To penetrate the City Centre. Passengers are no longer dumped at Victoria Station but can travel through to Market Street or other stations in the centre. Only those from Bury have a through journey but many from e.g. Rochdale and Oldham change at Victoria for the short tramway extension. Tickets to Victoria from any station in Greater Manchester are automatically valid into the City Centre as far as Piccadilly Station and G-Mex.
3. To breakdown the enormous psychological barrier, endemic in our country for at least 30/40 years, that trams are old fashioned, an impediment to the flow of traffic and unthinkable that they could ever return.

Statutory powers already exist for a number of extensions, one of which, to Salford Quays and Eccles, has opened in 1999/2000.

A long standing scheme has been for conversion of the Manchester–Oldham–Rochdale line. This would involve closure of the present diesel railway apart from freight access to Dean Lane. Trams would leave Manchester Victoria by the Bury line branching off at Irk Valley Junction to join the former 'loop line' at Smedley Viaduct Junction. They would cross over the Calder Valley main line at Thorpes Bridge Junction then assume the Oldham branch. Failsworth and Hollinwood stations would be replaced. There would be a deviation with street running through Oldham town centre returning to the railway alignment beyond Mumps. There would be interchange with the main line at Rochdale Station before continuing at street level into the town centre.

Statutory powers were granted in 1992 but the greater hurdle is finance. At the present rate of expansion (it has taken eight years to get the four miles to Eccles), the Oldham/Rochdale project might remain forever beyond the horizon. However, in March 2000 the Government announced support, subject to various caveats, for taking three Metrolink extensions forward together including Oldham/Rochdale. The other two are Wythenshaw/Manchester Airport and Ashton Under Lyne.

If the scheme goes ahead, it is inevitable that the Manchester–Oldham–Rochdale line will be out of use for a period. When it reopens in the new guise, there will be considerable benefits including a more frequent service and penetration of Oldham and Rochdale town centres. There will be drawbacks including longer journey times for some passengers. The proposed new service will not match the present 18 minute time from Manchester Victoria to Shaw & Crompton with only one stop. Instead it will be all stations via a low speed street section through the centre of Oldham.

8F 2-8-0 No. 48639 leaves New Hey on 20 June 1964 with a Saturday extra from Castleton to Penychain, the Butlins Holiday camp near Pwllheli. *(Ian G. Holt)*

An Aspinall 2-4-2T arriving at Milnrow with a Manchester to Rochdale train. A characteristic L&Y goods warehouse dominates the background.

(B.C. Lane collection)

WD 2-8-0 Nos. 90306 and 90141 are in charge of a pre-fabricated concrete-sleepered track relaying train on the Royton branch. The line on the left ascends to Higginshaw Gas Sidings.   *(J. Davenport)*

Outside Royton Station on 5 April 1920, a loaded 'flatbottom' is transferred from a horse drawn cart onto a motor lorry which is equipped with a hand winch behind the cab to effect the movement.

(B.C. Lane collection)

Wakes Week holiday traffic could bring prestige motive power on to the branch. 'Britannia' class 4-6-2 No. 70045 'Lord Rowallan' enters Shaw & Crompton with a Blackpool extra on 20 June 1964. *(Ian G. Holt)*

8F No. 48758 shunting at Royton Junction with an evening pick up goods from Oldham Mumps to Moston yard on 21 May 1967.
(Peter Hutchinson)

No. 1007 climbing from Victoria towards the City Centre on 25 May 1992. The roofboards proclaim 'It's great to be back'. *(Martin Bairstow)*

'Fairburn' 2-6-4T No. 42288 leaving Royton Junction on a Rochdale to Manchester train in June 1955. Aspinall 0-6-0 No. 52388 and a Fowler 7F 0-8-0 occupy the sidings.

(J. Davenport)

Aspinall 0-6-0 No. 52410, built in 1900, shunting at Shaw & Crompton in 1957. The view is towards Oldham.

(J. Davenport)

Middleton

A double track branch was opened to Middleton on 5 January 1857. One mile in length it left the main line north of Middleton Junction Station and descended at 1 in 85 and 1 in 80 from the junction.

In 1910 Middleton enjoyed 18 departures (8 on Sundays) mostly through to Manchester. By 1957 the number had declined to 6 on weekdays only. The introduction of dmus did not improve the frequency and the line closed to passengers on 5 September 1964 and to goods just over a year later.

A twin powered dmu has just taken the branch at Middleton Junction in September 1963. It is seen below awaiting departure from Middleton Station back to Manchester Victoria.   *(Ian G. Holt)*

Approaching Middleton Junction Station, Oldham branch platforms to right. Middleton trains used the main line platforms branching to the left at the far end of the station. *(H.C. Casserley)*

Fowler 2-6-2T No. 40015 has arrived at Middleton with a local from Manchester on 20 April 1951. *(H.C. Casserley)*

A Cravens dmu stands between the rotting canopies at Middleton on 13 January 1960. *(J.C.W. Halliday)*

Bacup

The highest summit on the Lancashire & Yorkshire Railway, 965 feet above sea level, was found just south of Britannia Station on the branch from Rochdale to Bacup. It was approached from both directions by gradients steeper than 1 in 40 and was rather exposed making the line one of the most scenic but difficult to work on the L&Y.

Drawn by the large number of mills in the valley and by the prospect of stone traffic from hillside quarries the Manchester & Leeds Railway had surveyed a route in 1845 and obtained powers for a Rochdale to Bacup branch in its Act of 1846 but these were allowed to lapse.

The branch as far as Facit was revived, despite some doubts amongst the L&Y Board, in 1861. An Act was obtained in June 1862 but work did not start until 1865. Difficulty was experienced in finding secure foundations for the 18 arch viaduct which carried the railway over the Roch Valley on the northern edge of Rochdale town centre. Problems were also encountered in stopping the banks of a cutting near Broadley from slipping. It took five years to complete the five mile branch which was eventually opened to goods on 5 October 1870 and to passengers on 1 November. The route was double track for the first mile and a quarter to Wardleworth which was a stone structure with canopies over the platforms. Beyond here there were extensive goods sidings but the branch continued as a single track on a steady climb around 1 in 60 through Shawclough & Healey Station, a single platform with a stone building. The site is now a housing estate but for the next 1 ½ miles to Whitworth the track bed has become a footpath. Access is thus available over the magnificent Healey Dell Viaduct which carried the railway 105 feet over the River Spodden flowing through the thickly wooded glen. The viaduct has eight stone arches plus an iron span over a road.

The extension from Facit to Bacup was authorised in 1872 and opened on 1 December 1881. It was built with double track. Approaching Shawforth, the line was carried above the adjacent road by a high retaining wall. The gradient from Facit to Britannia was mostly at 1 in 39 and 1 in 40. Once over the summit, the descent began at 1 in 34 and continued through a 144 yard tunnel past Bacup engine shed on the right to a junction with the East Lancashire Railway a short way before the island platform terminus.

The 1910 timetable is set out in full. Britannia Station became a First World War casualty in 1917. Other wartime cuts had mostly been restored by 1922 apart from the loss of the Sunday service and Saturday evening extras. These defects had been more than rectified in the 1938 timetable which offered 21 trains in each direction on Saturdays and quite a respectable Sunday service of seven trains commencing at midday and worked by a rail motor.

Rope worked inclines at both Facit and Britannia gave standard gauge access to the extensive sandstone quarries on Rooley Moor. At one time there was an interchange with a narrow gauge quarry line at Broadley Stone Siding. In later times this narrow gauge line was realigned to carry coal to Spring Mill Dyeworks.

The passenger service was 'temporarily suspended' by the LMS during a fuel crisis in June 1947 never to be resumed. After this the section from Facit to Bacup engine shed saw very little use. When the shed was closed in 1954 the junction at Bacup was lifted. Goods traffic, which included large quantities of raw asbestos to Turner's private siding at Shawclough, continued to reach Facit until 1963 when the branch was cut back to the coal yard at Whitworth. Complete closure followed in August 1967.

Aspinall 0-6-0 No. 52523 about to cross the Roch Valley between Rochdale and Wardleworth with a special on 28 July 1962.

(Ian G. Holt)

WEEKDAYS (Rochdale to Bacup)

Station	am	am	am	am	TFO am	am	am	pm	SO pm	pm	SO pm	pm	pm	SX pm	pm	pm	pm	pm	SO pm	SO pm	Sun am	Sun pm	Sun pm	Sun pm
ROCHDALE	5 50	7 07	8 15	9 08	9 47	10 32	11 15	12 10	12 35	1 33	1 50	3 05	4 20	5 06	5 35	6 38	8 42	9 20	10 10	10 48	8 55	4 12	8 20	10 10
WARDLEWORTH	5 53	7 10	8 18	9 11	9 50	10 35	11 18	12 13	12 38	1 36	1 53	3 08	4 23	5 09	5 38	6 41	8 45	9 23	10 13	10 51	8 58	4 16	8 24	10 14
SHAWCLOUGH & HEALEY	5 58	7 15		9 16		10 40	11 23			1 41	1 58	3 13	4 28		5 43	6 46	8 50	9 28	10 18	10 56	9 03	4 21	8 29	10 19
BROADLEY	6 02	7 19		9 20		10 44	11 27			1 45	2 02	3 17	4 32		5 47	6 50	8 54	9 32	10 22	11 00	9 07	4 26	8 34	10 24
WHITWORTH	6 05	7 22		9 23		10 47	11 30			1 48	2 05	3 20	4 35		5 50	6 53	8 57	9 35	10 25	11 03	9 10	4 31	8 39	10 29
FACIT	6 09	7 26		9 27		10 51	11 34			1 52	2 09	3 24	4 39		5 54	6 57	9 01	9 39	10 29	11 07	9 14	4 36	8 44	10 34
SHAWFORTH	6 14	7 31		9 32		10 56	11 39			1 57	2 14	3 29	4 44		5 59	7 02	9 06	9 44	10 34	11 12	9 19	4 42	8 50	10 40
BRITANNIA	6 18	7 35		9 36		11 00	11 43			2 01	2 18	3 33	4 48		6 03	7 06	9 10	9 48	10 38	11 16	9 23	4 46	8 54	10 44
BACUP	6 22	7 39		9 40		11 04	11 47			2 05	2 22	3 37	4 52		6 09	7 10	9 14	9 52	10 42	11 21	9 27	4 50	8 58	10 48

WEEKDAYS (Bacup to Rochdale)

Station	am	am	am	am	am	TFO am	am	am	SO pm	SO pm	pm	pm	pm	SX pm	pm	pm	pm	pm	SO pm	SO pm	Sun am	Sun pm	Sun pm	Sun pm
BACUP		6 42	7 20	8 02		9 35		11 25		12 45	2 03	2 39	3 52		5 45	6 47	7 32	8 55	9 45	11 00	8 30	1 50	6 40	9 15
BRITANNIA		6 47	7 25	8 07		9 40		11 30		12 50	2 08	2 44	3 57		5 50	6 52	7 37	9 00	9 50	11 05	8 35	1 55	6 45	9 20
SHAWFORTH		6 50	7 28	8 10		9 43		11 33		12 53	2 11	2 47	4 00		5 53	6 55	7 40	9 03	9 53	11 08	8 38	1 58	6 48	9 23
FACIT		6 53	7 31	8 13		9 46		11 36		12 56	2 14	2 50	4 03		5 56	6 58	7 43	9 06	9 56	11 11	8 41	2 01	6 51	9 26
WHITWORTH		6 56	7 34	8 16		9 49		11 39		12 59	2 17	2 53	4 06		5 59	7 01	7 46	9 09	9 59	11 14	8 44	2 04	6 54	9 29
BROADLEY		6 59	7 37	8 19		9 52		11 42		1 02	2 20	2 56	4 09		6 02	7 04	7 49	9 12	10 02	11 17	8 47	2 07	6 57	9 32
SHAWCLOUGH & HEALEY		7 03	7 41	8 23		9 56		11 46		1 06	2 24	3 00	4 13		6 06	7 08	7 53	9 16	10 06	11 21	8 51	2 11	7 01	9 36
WARDLEWORTH	4 45	7 09	7 47	8 29	9 18	10 02	10 45	11 52	12 25	1 06	2 24	3 00	4 19	5 36	6 12	7 14	7 59	9 22	10 12	11 27	8 57	2 17	7 07	9 42
ROCHDALE	4 50	7 12	7 50	8 32	9 21	10 05	10 48	11 55	12 28	1 15	2 33	3 09	4 22	5 39	6 15	7 17	8 02	9 25	10 15	11 30	9 00	2 20	7 10	9 45

TFO = TUESDAYS AND FRIDAYS ONLY.   SO = SATURDAYS ONLY.   SX = SATURDAYS EXCEPTED.

APRIL 1910

LANCASHIRE & YORKSHIRE RAILWAY.
Issued subject to the regulations and conditions in the Co's Time Tables, Books, Bills and Notices. Available on day of issue only.
THIRD CLASS
BACUP TO
ROCHDALE
216
Rochdale   Fare 8½d

Wardleworth box was a standard L&Y timber design but this particular example stood on girders over the track. It had 40 levers, was opened in 1899 and was No. 243 in the L&Y lists. It closed in August 1967.
(Ian G. Holt)

4F 0-6-0 No. 44096 pulls out of Shawclough & Healey in order to set back into Turners Siding on 10 December 1960.
(Ian G. Holt)

Broadley was visited by a track recording trolley on 28 August 1961. *(Ian G. Holt)*

D3845 worked the last train to Whitworth on 19 August 1967. *(Ian G. Holt)*

Shawforth Station looking towards Bacup in 1955. The desolate stretch between Facit and Bacup had fallen into disuse by this time. *(F. W. Shuttleworth)*

44096 shunting at Shawclough & Healey on 10 December 1960. The view is towards Bacup. *(Ian G. Holt)*

On 19 February 1967, ex L&Y 0-4-0 ST No 51218, now preserved on the Keighley & Worth Valley Railway, operated three brake van trips between Rochdale and Whitworth. It is seen heading across Healey Dell Viaduct on the outward journey.

(Ian G. Holt)

Yorkshire Branch Lines

A Hughes railmotor emerges from Ripponden Tunnel, Sowerby Bridge, in the early 1920s bound for Rishworth.
(B.C. Lane collection)

Rishworth

When the Lancashire & Yorkshire Railway submitted plans for a branch into the Ryburn Valley, it was not just looking at the small traffic centres of Ripponden and Rishworth, but to the more exciting prospect of continuing beyond the head of the valley, through a long tunnel beneath Blackstone Edge so as to rejoin the existing main line near Rochdale. The distance from Sowerby Bridge to Rochdale would have been reduced by five miles. Parliamentary powers were obtained in 1865 for a line from Sowerby Bridge to Ripponden but progress was slow due to the railway having heavy commitments elsewhere. The five years allowed for completion were extended in 1868 and again in 1870 by an Act which also extended the line to Rishworth. Work began in 1873 but difficulties were experienced in constructing the tunnel near the start of the branch at Sowerby Bridge and there were landslips in the Triangle area. The Company considered a Parliamentary bill to allow deviations to the route in 1876, but dropped this when outstanding problems were overcome. It still took two years to complete the line as far as Ripponden which was opened to goods traffic on 1 July 1878, and to passengers on 5 August. The extension to Rishworth opened on 1 March 1881.

In anticipation of the opening of the branch, a new station was built at Sowerby Bridge to the east of the previous structure. Opened on 1 September 1876, the main buildings were set in the angle of the junction and tend to confirm the intention that this would be the divergence of two main lines. The failure to provide any platforms on the branch suggests that the Company saw little prospect for the Rishworth line unless it was extended. The branch trains had to propel from a short bay platform back to the junction before setting forward for Rishworth. The line was of double track and would have been capable of sustaining high speed running, being free of sharp curves. The largest engineering feature was the 593 yard Ripponden Tunnel near Sowerby Bridge. The branch was laid on the east side of the valley on an almost continuous rising gradient, starting at 1 in 107 and

increasing to 1 in 60 beyond Triangle where a station was opened in 1885. The single platform terminus at Rishworth was a little short of the village from which access was gained by a steep viaduct, built in timber but paved in sets for the benefit of horse drawn vehicles.

Progress with the main line extension never got beyond the preliminary planning stage, presumably because of capital commitments elsewhere on the L&Y system. The branch settled down to a quiet existence and in later years was worked on one track only, the other being used as a siding to store carriages. On 16 August 1926, a train of empty carriages started moving from Ripponden and had a domino effect on other sets which were stabled at various points on the branch. A total of 112 carriages were involved and were only stopped when the front ones became derailed by a catch point before the tunnel. The first eight were destroyed, their progress down the branch having been witnessed by passengers on a Sowerby Bridge to Rishworth train which had passed them near Triangle.

Stainland

The 1¾ mile branch from Greetland (then called North Dean) was authorised in 1865 by the same Act as the line to Ripponden. Its history closely follows the pattern of its neighbour. Progress in building was only marginally faster and it took until 1 January 1875 for opening to be achieved. The first passenger trains operated only to and from North Dean but some were soon extended to Halifax. The branch was built double track and crossed two substantial viaducts. That at West Vale consisted of 13 arches and was 230 yards long, whilst Stainland Viaduct was 179 yards long and of 14 arches. The intermediate station of West Vale had two platforms on a sharp curve but Stainland & Holywell Green had only one. The gradient was 1 in 50 for most of the way rising towards Stainland. The terminus was at Holywell Green a mile short of the village of Stainland which is at a much higher altitude.

Railmotor No. 4 poses for the camera at the inauguration of the Stainland service in 1907.

(Roy Brook collection)

Tramways and railmotors

In 1898 Halifax Corporation embarked upon the construction of a 3ft 6in gauge electric tramway network. Serving the centre of the town as well as Halifax Old Station this new form of transport was well suited to take short distance traffic from the railways but the effect of tramway competition must not be over emphasised. In West Yorkshire, although tramway coverage was very comprehensive by the first decade of the century, the various municipalities failed to adopt a common gauge and ruled themselves out of the market for inter-urban transport. A journey from Bradford to Huddersfield involved three different gauges, none of them standard. A tramway was opened to Triangle on 7 February 1905, and unlike the trains, the trams ran through to Halifax. West Vale was served by Halifax trams from 2 August 1905 and also by a line from Huddersfield from 1914. It was not until 14 May 1921, that the tramway was extended from West Vale to Holywell Green (near the station) and thence up the hill to Stainland itself. The Halifax Tramway system is included on the map of Calderdale both to explain the extent to which it competed with the railways and to give an impression of the size of the combined network when both forms of rail transport were at their fullest extent.

Whether moved by tramway competition or just by a desire to improve branch line operations, the L&Y introduced a more frequent service on 1 March 1907, from Sowerby Bridge to Rishworth and from Halifax to Stainland. The motive power was a rail motor, a single coach combined with a small locomotive. Additional rail level halts were opened at Rochdale Road and Watsons Crossing, and a short platform was provided on the branch at Sowerby Bridge Station. Tickets were issued on the train which was third class only.

By the late 1920s both branches were suffering competition from the then unregulated bus services. The Rishworth line was particularly vulnerable as each station, whilst not spectacularly remote, was a longer walk from the village than the main road. Buses operated to Halifax town centre whilst the rail passenger had to change at Sowerby Bridge in order to reach the Old Station at the bottom of the town. The LMS and LNER obtained powers to enter the bus industry joining the Corporation in forming the Halifax Joint Omnibus Committee in 1929. They decided that it was better to have control over the buses which could connect with trains at Sowerby Bridge rather than to persevere with the branch trains and face private bus competition. The Rishworth passenger service ended on Saturday 6 July 1929, the rail motor becoming derailed after discharging its last passengers at Sowerby Bridge and blocking the main line until Sunday morning.

The Stainland closure followed on 21 September. The tramways themselves fell victim to the Halifax Joint Omnibus Committee, and both the Triangle and Stainland lines closed during 1934. Goods traffic was carried by the branch railways until the 1950s. The viaducts at West Vale and Stainland remain as landmarks and much of the Rishworth track bed is still visible.

The rail level platform at
Watsons Crossing Halt,
looking towards Rishworth.
(Alan Young collection)

Ripponden & Barkisland
looking towards Rishworth.
The railmotor will have
crossed over from the 'up'
line to the 'down' at the
entrance to the station.
(Alan Young collection)

The 14 arch Stainland Viaduct
is still in existence more than
40 years after the track was
removed. The railmotor
appears to be running with
the trailer leading towards
Halifax.
(Martin Bairstow collection)

Hughes railmotor No. 1 paired with carriage No. 1 from the original Kerr Stuart railcar which it replaced in 1909. It is seen at Watsons Crossing Halt which had only a rail level platform.
(B.C. Lane collection)

A later photo of a Kerr Stuart railcar rebuilt after the Great War with a corridor connection.
(B.C. Lane collection)

Railmotor No. 1 at Triangle with the other track in use for carriage storage.
(B.C. Lane collection)

No. 3 at Rishworth about 1911.
(B.C. Lane collection)

The branch terminus at Stainland & Holywell Green looking towards the buffer stops. *(B.C. Lane collection)*

Halifax tram No. 67 standing at the Triangle terminus. The route was restricted to open top cars due to the low railway bridge at Sowerby Bridge.
(Roy Brook collection)

The Spen Valley Line

The branch from Mirfield to Low Moor was amongst the West Riding Lines authorised on 18 August 1846 and was the first section to be completed. Opened on 12 July 1848, the railway was brought within three miles of Bradford and a horse drawn omnibus connection was provided. From 9 May 1850 the trains were able to run through to Bradford itself.

Low Moor was then the scene of heavy industry. The final stage of the railway journey through the Spen Valley was described by the 'Halifax Guardian' in its report on the opening: 'The lovely vale of Cleckheaton, and the distant hills covered with wood are then lost sight of and with seeming appropriateness a short tunnel introduces the traveller to the dirty smoky chimneys which day and night vomit forth alternate blasts of fire and smoke at the Low Moor and Bierley Ironworks. A more complete change of scenery and a more dingy sight can scarcely be imagined. Instead of the verdant landscape and smiling pastures, there are on every hand immense accumulations of the debris of the iron and coal mines which abound in the locality, the bleak ground being filled by the village like works of Low Moor and each tall chimney apparently striving to pour out a greater amount of fire and smoke than its neighbour'.

Thomas Normington was a guard based at Mirfield in the early 1850s and tells of operating difficulties one Saturday evening in July 1853. Working the last Huddersfield to Bradford train he suffered an engine failure at Low Moor. There was no other motive power available and no telegraph so he uncoupled one carriage and harnessed to it a horse which he then had walked through Bowling Tunnel to Bowling Junction whence he 'drove' the train by gravity to Bradford where he claims he was applauded by his passengers. He then had to walk back to Mirfield accompanied by a traveller who was in the habit of riding home on the light engine—a service no available that night.

Leaving the Manchester & Leeds Railway at Cleckheaton Junction just east of Mirfield Station the branch soon crossed the Calder & Hebble Navigation by

Northorpe North Road, likened by Thomas Normington to a Bishop's Palace rather than a railway station.

(G. C. Lewthwaite)

A Huddersfield to Bradford dmu passing the original Heckmondwike Station building latterly used as a goods office. The 1888 island platform is beyond. (Peter E. Baughan)

timber bridge, replaced by an iron span in 1882. After a fairly level run to Heckmondwike, there was then a five mile climb at 1 in 100 to Low Moor.

The first station, at Northorpe, was not opened until 1891. Its facilities were adequate, at least in the opinion of Thomas Normington who thought the architecture more fitted to a Bishop's Palace than a Railway Station.'

Approaching Heckmondwike the line passed under a skew girder bridge on the LNWR 'Leeds New Line' then joined the L&Y route from Thornhill at Heckmondwike Junction. The station was an island platform with access by a subway from the booking office which was at street level. The station opened on this site on 9 August 1888 replacing a structure a little to the south.

Liversedge station was rebuilt in 1884/85 but on the same site, the platforms being extended southwards under the road bridge which replaced a level crossing.

Cleckheaton became an island platform in 1881 with access from the roadway below. There were loops on either side of the passenger lines through the station and an extensive goods yard. North of Cleckheaton there were sidings for the gas works and tar distillers.

The Heckmondwike and Dewsbury Branches

Branches from Thornhill to Heckmondwike and Dewsbury were also authorised in 1846 but left in abeyance until they were revived in the 1860s after the L&Y had failed to reach agreement with the LNWR for a cheaper alternative. This would have involved creating triangular junctions at Cleckheaton Junction (Mirfield) and at Thornhill LNWR Junction by the construction of north to east curves to allow trains to run from Bradford via the Spen Valley to Dewsbury Wellington Road and from there to Wakefield Kirkgate.

The refusal of the LNWR to accommodate such services in its Dewsbury station led to the L&Y going ahead with its independent line into Dewsbury Market Place. One mile in length the branch left the Calder Valley by a double junction east of Thornhill and terminated at a covered island platform with an extensive goods yard. Goods traffic began in 27 August 1866 and from 1 April 1867 there were passenger trains from Dewsbury to Wakefield and to Mirfield. This latter service was replaced by one to Bradford Exchange on 1 June 1869 when the Thornhill to Heckmondwike branch opened. This crossed under the LNWR by a bridge which was actually built in anticipation when the LNWR line itself was under construction in 1847. It then immediately crosses the Calder by a 12 arch stone viaduct. The sole intermediate station was at Ravensthorpe.

In 1882, the Great Northern Railway promoted a bill for a branch from Dewsbury to Heckmondwike, Liversedge and Cleckheaton which was opposed by the L&Y. The result was a compromise involving a few short curves and an exchange of running powers to make better use of existing routes. The GNR was to build short links between Hare Park and Crofton West Junctions (giving access from Kings Cross to Wakefield Kirkgate) from Headfield Junction to Dewsbury Junction (giving access from the Calder Valley to Dewsbury Central), and from Pudsey Greenside via Dudley Hill to Low Moor (giving a shorter route from Leeds to the Spen Valley). The L&Y was to build the south curve at Low Moor enabling Great Northern trains to run from Wakefield to Halifax via Thornhill and Cleckheaton. This joint L&Y/GN effort culminated in the introduction on 1 December 1893 of a circular service from Leeds Central via Pudsey, Low Moor, the Spen Valley, Thornhill, Dewsbury Central, Batley, Beeston and back to Leeds Central.

Heckmondwike Station before 1888 looking towards Mirfield. The track had been temporarily singled whilst an underbridge was built between this and the new station site.
(B.C. Lane collection)

The 1889 station at Heckmondwike was an island platform reached by a subway from the booking office which was at road level.
(Martin Bairstow collection)

The 2.25 pm Huddersfield to Bradford restarts from Liversedge on 19 October 1962 and immediately enters the short Littletown Tunnel.
(Peter E. Baughan)

The Spen Valley line was occasionally used as a diversionary route. Class 40 No. D354 passing through Cleckheaton with 'The White Rose' from Kings Cross to Bradford and Leeds.
(Martin Bairstow collection)

A Fowler 2-6-4T restarts from Cleckheaton with a Huddersfield to Bradford service in August 1959. The coaching stock embraces LNW, GN and LMS patterns.

(Peter Sunderland)

The passenger terminal at Dewsbury Market Place, closed 1930 and demolished 1938/9.

(Lancashire & Yorkshire Railway Society)

The Spen Valley line joined the route from Halifax in Low Moor Station.

(B.C. Lane collection)

Aspinall 0-6-0 No. 52121 shunting Thornhill goods yard on 2 April 1960. The view is towards Wakefield.

(J.C.W. Halliday)

Ex L&Y 0-6-0 No. 52515 at Dewsbury Market Place on 2 April 1960. The 54 year old engine then had two further years to run. The branch was just ten months from final closure. *(J.C.W. Halliday)*

BRADFORD EXCHANGE TO DEWSBURY AND HUDDERSFIELD VIA CLECKHEATON

(April 1910 timetable — up direction only)

WEEKDAYS	am	am	am	am	am	am	am	am	am	am	am	am	am	pm	pm	pm	pm	pm	pm	pm	pm	pm	pm	pm	pm	pm	pm
BRADFORD EXCHANGE		5 50	6 38	7 20	7 35	7 45		8 40	9 10	9 45	10 38		11 20	12 02	12 13		1 05	1 40		2 43	3 20	3 50	4 25		5 03	5 25
OWLING JUNCTION		5 55	6 43	7 25	—	7 52		8 45	9 15	9 50	—		11 25	—	12 18		1 10	1 45		2 48	—	3 55	—		—	5 30
LEEDS CENTRAL							8 00				10 40															
LOW MOOR	5 30	6 00	6 49	7 30	7A 43	7 58	8 33	8 51	9 20	9 55	10 47	11 09	11 30	12A10	12 23		1 15	1 50		2 53	3A29	4 03	4 33		5 11	5 35
CLECKHEATON	5 36	6 06	6 55	7 37	7A 49	8 04	8 39	8 57	9 26	10 01	10 53	11 15	11 36	12A16	12 29	12 39	2 11	1 56	2 11	2 59	3A35	4 09	4 39	5 03	5 17	5 41
LIVERSEDGE	5 39	6 09	6 58	7 41	7A 51	8 08	8 42	9 00	9 29	10 04	10 56	11 18	11 39	12A19	12 32	12 42	2 41	1 59	2 17	3 02	3A38	4 12	4 42	5 06	5 23	5 47
HECKMONDWIKE	5 42	6 12	7 01	7 45	7A 54	8 11	8 45	9 03	9 32	10 07	10 59	11 21	11 42	12A23	12 35	12 45	1 27	2 02	2 17	3 05	3A42	4 15	4 45	5 09	5 25	5 47
RAVENSTHORPE	6 17					8 16	8 50		9 37	10 12		11 26			12 40	12 49		2 07			4 20			5 14	5 28	
THORNHILL	6 19				8A10	8 21	8 53		9 40	10 14		11 29		12A37	12 42	12 52		2 09	2 23		3A53	4 23		5 16	5 30	
DEWSBURY MARKET PL	6 24					8 25			9 45	10 19				12 47				2 14							5 35	
DEWSBURY CENTRAL					8 57						11 33															
NORTHORPE	5 46		7 05	7 49			9 07				11 03		11 46			1 31			3 09			4 49			5 51	
MIRFIELD	5 50		7 08	7 56			9 14				11 08		11 53			1 36			3 15			4 54			5 56	
HUDDERSFIELD	6 00			8 06			9 26				11 20		12 03						3 23			5 07			6 06	

WEEKDAYS	pm	pm	pm	pm	pm	pm	pm	pm	pm	pm	pm	SX	SO		SUNDAYS am	am	am	pm	pm	pm	pm	pm	pm	pm	pm
BRADFORD EXCHANGE		5 52	6 00	6 20		6 53		7 50	8 25	9 30	10 30	11 22	11 35		9 05	9 45	11 05		1 55	2 55	5 25	6 15	8 35	9 05	
OWLING JUNCTION			6 05	6 26		6 58		7 55	—	10 35	—				9 10	9 50	11 10		2 00	3 00	5 30	6 20	8 40	9 13	
LEEDS CENTRAL	5 10						7 37											12 40							9 40
LOW MOOR	5 38	6A00	6 10	6 30		7 03		8 00	8 33	38	10 40	11 30	11 43		9 15	9 56	11 15	12 12	2 06	3 05	5 36	6 27	8 46	9 18	10 19
CLECKHEATON	5 44	6A06	6 16	6 36	6 55	7 09	7 57	8 06	8 39	9 44	10 46	11 36	11 49		9 21	10 02	11 21	18	2 12	3 11	5 42	6 33	8 52	9 24	10 19
LIVERSEDGE	5 47	6A09	6 19	6 39	6 58	7 12	8 02	8 09	8 42	9 47	10 49	11 39	11 52		9 24	10 05	11 24	21	2 15	3 14	5 45	6 36	8 55	9 27	10 22
HECKMONDWIKE	5 50	6A11	6 22	6 42	7 01	7 15	8 03	8 12	8 45	9 50	10 52	11 42	11 55		9 27	10 08	11 27	24	2 18	3 17	5 48	6 39	8 58	9 30	10 25
RAVENSTHORPE	5 55	—	6 27			7 06		8 17	8 50		10 57	12 00			10 13		1 29		3 22	5 53			9 35	10 30	
THORNHILL	5 58	6A27	6 37			7 08		8 19	8 52		10 59	12 02			10 15		1 32		3 24	5 55			9 46	10 33	
DEWSBURY MARKET PL	—		6 42			7 13		8 24	8 57		11 05	12 06			10 20				3 29	6 00			9 51		
DEWSBURY CENTRAL	6 02																37								10 37
NORTHORPE			6 46		7 19	8 07		9 54							9 34	11 31		2 22			6 50	9 02			
MIRFIELD			6 52		7 22	8 11		9 58								11 35		2 27			6 59	9 06			
HUDDERSFIELD			7 02															2 37			7 00				

A - STOPS TO PICK UP FOR SHEFFIELD AND BEYOND.   SO = SATURDAYS ONLY.   SX = SATURDAYS EXCEPTED

APRIL 1910

The full 1910 timetable is set out for the up direction only. Already the circular service from Leeds had declined in frequency following opening of the LNWR 'Leeds New' line in 1900. It stopped altogether at the end of August 1914. The Low Moor to Dudley Hill line fell into disuse in 1917 and the GNR decided to salvage the track.

With three passenger stations, Dewsbury was an obvious candidate for rationalisation and Market Place closed in 1930 although freight continued to use the branch for another 31 years.

Trains between Bradford and Wakefield declined in number, the last one being withdrawn in 1957. At that time there were just nine trains from Bradford to Huddersfield via the Spen Valley plus a couple of extras on Saturdays and nothing on Sundays.

When diesel multiple units were introduced in November 1959, the long gaps between trains were filled to give almost an hourly service. With a similar frequency also operating via Halifax, there was virtually a train every half hour from Bradford to Huddersfield. This arrangement was short lived and by 1962 gaps had reappeared in the timetable. In June 1965 the service was withdrawn completely from both routes.

The line between Heckmondwike and Mirfield was closed to all traffic but that between Low Moor and Thornhill remained available for freight. Traffic north of Heckmondwike was negligible and the line was severed between Cleckheaton and Low Moor in 1970 when the motorway was under construction. It reopened in 1974 with a new viaduct but hardly any trains, finally closing in 1981.

A single track remained in use from Thornhill to Heckmondwike where it had been connected since 1966 to a section of the ex LNWR 'Leeds New Line' to give access to an oil terminal near Liversedge Spen but this closed in 1986. All the way from Low Moor, the track remained in situ until the late 1990s when most of the route was turned into a cycle path.

The link between Headfield Junction and Dewsbury (GN), closed since 1933, was reopened in 1965. The track is still in place from Dewsbury East Junction but has been disused since 1990 except for access to the cement works.

The Pickle Bridge Branch
Neither the Halifax nor Cleckheaton routes provided a particularly direct line from Bradford to Huddersfield. The L&Y had two alternatives to remedy this both of which had featured among the West Riding lines abandoned in the early 1850s. A railway from Elland to Huddersfield with a tunnel under Ainley top would have kept Halifax on the direct route and with hindsight it may seem a pity that this was not the option chosen.

Instead in response to a threatened incursion into its territory by other railways, the L&Y pressed ahead with the line from Pickle Bridge, on the Bradford-Halifax line, to Anchor Pit Junction east of Brighouse.

Authorised in 1865 but amended by a further Act of 1873, the work finally started in 1874. The principal engineering feature was the 270 yard long viaduct at Wyke which, along with the sharp curve off the Halifax line was made necessary by the failure to purchase land on the original planned route.

Opening took place on 1 March 1881, the same day as the line to Rishworth. Pickle Bridge Station, renamed Wyke in 1882, was moved a little way towards Bradford on 23 September 1896 when its name was extended to embrace Norwood Green.

Leaving the Calder Valley by a sharp curve at Anchor Pit Junction the branch climbed at 1 in 60 for most of the first mile to Clifton Road Station which served Brighouse. Between here and Bailiff Bridge there were two viaducts each of four arches. Continuing to climb mainly at 1 in 70 the line was carried over the 22 arch Wyke Viaduct to reach the Halifax line just south of Wyke Station.

Bailiff Bridge Station was one of the 'temporary' closures of 1917 when railway staff were in short supply due to the numbers engaged in rather less peaceful duties in Flanders. Like many of them, Bailiff Bridge did not return. Clifton Road closed in 1931 after which few passenger trains used the route. These were diverted in 1948 and total closure followed in 1952 due to the condition of Wyke Viaduct.

The lines downfall was that, although it was the shortest of three routes between Bradford and Huddersfield, it served the least intermediate population.

It did however gain 'main line' status in 1900 when a Bradford Exchange — Marylebone service was routed this way then via Huddersfield and Penistone. Taking five hours, the 'South Yorkshireman' as it was later known, ran until 1960 but latterly via Halifax.

If one examines the lie of the land between Wyke Tunnel and the Bailiff Bridge end of the viaduct, it is easy to see the route which the railway could have adopted avoiding both the structure and the low speed junction. In 1986 BR posted notices on the 'unnecessary' viaduct seeking listed building consent to demolish it.

An Aspinall 0-6-0 enters Bailiff Bridge with a Bradford to Huddersfield local. The wooden platforms were reached by a white tiled subway from the booking office at road level.
(B.C. Lane collection)

Clifton Road Station looking towards Bradford.
(R. Wade collection)

Legal History

Had the new Heckmondwike Station been ready just over a year earlier, the Lancashire & Yorkshire Railway could have saved £396 in damages plus substantial legal costs.

On 14 May 1887, a Mrs Wharton travelled with her three children from Cleckheaton to Heckmondwike. At that time, Cleckheaton had high platforms but Heckmondwike was still the old station with a 3 foot drop from the floor of the carriage to the platform. There were two continuous footboards on the carriage. One was 11½ inches below the floor projecting outwards by 6 inches. The other was 17½ inches further down but was inset by comparison with the higher step and therefore invisible from inside the train.

Mrs Wharton claimed not to have visited Heckmondwike Station for ten years. It hadn't changed but she was not familiar with it.

The train reached Heckmondwike at 5.15pm in full daylight. The three children jumped out. Mrs Wharton, clasping a small bag in one hand and the window strap with the other, managed to put one foot on the footboard. As she attempted to reach the platform with her other foot, she fell forward breaking her right knee cap and sustaining other injuries.

She sued the Railway before Mr Justice Charles, sitting with a jury in York. The jury awarded £396 in damages. However, the learned judge doubted whether there was sufficient evidence of negligence for the question of damages to have been put to the jury. He left each party to apply for judgement in the Divisional Court where Mr Justice Field and Mr Justice Willis found in favour of the Railway Company.

Mrs Wharton then appealed to the Court of Appeal before the Master of the Rolls, Lord Esher sitting with Lord Justices Fry and Lopes. Both sides were represented by Queen's Counsel.

The Master of the Rolls said that the case would have been clear but for the decision of the Divisional Court (which he possibly found surprising). Lord Justice Lopes intervened to prevent Counsel for Mrs Wharton making a speech on the history of negligence. 'Such a thing', he said, was totally unnecessary.

There was legal precedent that the Railway must 'afford reasonable facilities for alighting' and that the train coming to a stand in the station was 'an invitation to alight'. Counsel for the Railway claimed that his client had afforded reasonable facilities and that Mrs Wharton had caused her own misfortune by attempting to get out without asking for assistance. 'She saw the risk she ran and she elected to run the risk. She saw every element of danger'.

The Railway suggested that she could have alighted backwards and felt for the second step to help herself down. The Court was not swayed by that argument. Mrs Wharton said that she had looked for a porter but could not see one.

The Court held that a Railway Company knew it had to carry passengers of different ages and degrees of agility including women who might be impeded by long dresses. It did not 'afford reasonable facilities for alighting' if 'a large class of passengers' were unable to manage without calling for assistance. The Company could have posted notices warning of the danger in not seeking assistance but they had not done so. The Court recognised that passengers must get off quickly before the train sets off again. Lord Justice Fry noted evidence that a large number of stations on the Lancashire & Yorkshire Railway had platforms similar to Heckmondwike. He advised the Company that the sooner they altered the level of the platforms, the better it would be for them.

The appeal was allowed thus confirming the jury's award of £396 and presumably causing the Railway to meet both sides' costs. £396 would be worth nearly £50,000 in today's money.

The case was hardly a landmark event. Mrs Wharton, or her husband, must have had considerable funds with which to finance the action. Access to justice then was the privilege of only a few. Nowadays, one imagines that a Railway Company, or its insurer, would try to settle out of Court. The Lancashire & Yorkshire Railway might well have found such a course cheaper.

Liversedge Station with low platforms prior to the 1894 rebuilding when the level crossing in the foreground was replaced by the bridge which appears on page 96.
(Martin Bairstow collection)

Running Lines – A Station Masters Story

By Les Hoyle

Liversedge Station looking towards Huddersfield. The buildings on the right are part of the original station to which access was from a level crossing. In 1884/85, this was replaced by a road bridge, the platforms were extended under it and the new booking office was at road level.

(Peter E. Baughan)

I returned from national service in the Royal Navy in March 1948 only to find that my post as photographer for the *Cleckheaton and Spenborough Guardian* had been reclaimed by its former occupant on his return from regular duty in the armed forces. I had been out of work for a while when I learned there was a vacancy for a porter at Heckmondwike Central. I visited the station to obtain an application form and found the clerk on duty there was a former Heckmondwike Grammar School pupil like myself. I was persuaded by him to apply for a clerical post instead of the porter's job.

Shortly afterward, I was asked to attend for interview and an aptitude test at the District Managers' Office located in the large house below Wakefield Westgate station also used for many years as the Wakefield control offices. On 12 June 1948 I was informed that I had been appointed a trainee booking clerk and was requested to report for training at Liversedge Central Station on the London Midland Region (former L&Y) at 0900 Monday 17 June 1948. So began a career on the railway somewhat unintentionally, but which was to last for more than 35 years.

Liversedge Central was on the Cleckheaton Branch served by trains between Bradford Exchange and Huddersfield via Low Moor and Mirfield. It comprised two platforms, Up and Down, with a booking office above at road level. Access to the platforms was by a wooden overbridge with staircases on each side. The stationmaster at that time was Bernard Horsman who was also the Goods Agent responsible for the coal yard (down side) and the freight shed and sidings (up side). The goods office was located on the up platform next door to his office.

On reporting to Mr Horsman I was introduced to the booking clerk on duty with whom I was hoping to work opposite shifts once trained. I found to my surprise yet another ex schoolmate Peter Wildman.

Peter undertook my training with the same enthusiasm he displayed towards all railway matters. He was so keen that he subscribed to the monthly edition of *Bradshaw* and took it to bed for light reading. He ordered tickets which were never issued including Liversedge to Douglas, Isle of Man, second class rail/first class steamer. The Edmondson card ticket had a little pull out section for the first class upgrade. Peter emigrated to Rhodesia and was replaced by another ex schoolmate, Bob Smith. He was later to become stationmaster at Addingham and, eventually, ASM at Birmingham New Street.

The clerical duties comprised sale of passenger tickets, parcels, luggage collection sheets and delivery sheets for the parcels and goods delivery agents.

At Heckmondwike Central, goods and parcels were delivered by Railway owned Scammell three wheeled vehicles, but at Liversedge the work was contracted to a firm call Ramsden's who employed a horse and cart.

I had only been working a short time at Liversedge when, to the surprise of all members of staff, the painters arrived to paint the station for the first time in living memory. At that time the Midland colours were the famous plum and spilt milk and the station looked really nice upon completion. However, contemporarily with this a relocation of Regional boundaries was taking place. We had already been asked if we wished to opt for Midland or Eastern identity, as Liversedge was to be embraced within the new Eastern Region boundary. It will come as no surprise that Bob and I opted for Eastern, principally to ensure that we stayed where we were at Liversedge until things at least settled down.

Surprise was an understatement when, within a fortnight of completion of the Midland painting, along came the Eastern painters who proceeded to paint everything they could see with LNER green, including the beautiful mahogany desk tops in the booking office and the inset brass handles which had been so lovingly polished for generations. This garish colour made the old triangular sink in the corner of the office seem even more in need of replacement. Repeated requests to our stationmaster had always been turned down on the grounds of cost. Bob and I managed accidentally to drop the cast iron fire kettle in it and in due course we got our new sink.

The early turn clerk at Liversedge was required to travel to Cleckheaton Central two mornings each week to assist with claims work for Sugdens Shirts and Phelon & Moore Motorcycles (Panther) who were the principal customers for parcels by passenger train from Cleckheaton. At this time, 1949/50, the 'South Yorkshireman' was running between Bradford and London Marylebone via Low Moor, Cleckheaton, Huddersfield and Sheffield. The train did not have a booked stop at Cleckheaton but would call on request if there were passengers wishing to join. Unfortunately the signal layout at Cleckheaton North meant that the train had already passed the starting signal whilst still approaching the up platform which was actually in the section between Cleckheaton and Liversedge signal boxes. In order to achieve the request stop, the porter was despatched some 300 yards from the station to stand on the top of the permanent way salt box and wave a red flag at the driver, a system I have never known since in my entire railway career.

The three Stationmasters at Liversedge Central, Cleckheaton Central and Heckmondwike Central were also respectively in charge at Liversedge Spen, Cleckheaton Spen and Heckmondwike Spen on the LNW Line between Huddersfield and Leeds. Staffing at these stations comprised only a leading porter on early and late turns. The early turn man paid all receipts in daily at Central booking office. The leading porter at Liversedge Spen also recorded wagon arrivals and departures at the goods yard where traffic was mainly wagons of coal and some scrap etc. These sidings were later used as an oil tanker depot but are now lost beneath a housing development.

During 1949/50 I was privileged to befriend the signalman at Liversedge Central box, who introduced me to such mysteries as absolute block, single line working and the Rules and Regulations. It is probably due to him that I set my sights on a stationmaster's career. Evening classes in passenger and goods station work resulted in a qualification that allowed

me to apply, perhaps cheekily, for a Summer relief station master's post (class 4) during early 1951. I was appointed to a post based at Laisterdyke in March 1951 and sent to Wakefield Westgate to learn North Eastern paybills. In fact I never set foot on Laisterdyke Station, being used as relief out of Wakefield Westgate for the rest of the summer. During this time I relieved at local stations including Alverthorpe, Tingley, Lofthouse, Hemsworth, St Dunstans, Holmfield, incorporating Ovenden and Halifax North Bridge and as ASM Westgate.

During the summer, I was scanning the vacancy list to try for a permanent stationmasters job rather than sink back into obscurity at Liversedge. I applied for and got an interview for stationmaster (class 5) at Wyke & Norwood Green. I was successful following a stringent oral and written examination at Hunts Bank Offices, Manchester in rules and regulations, block working, single line, passenger and goods working. I was appointed to the post at a wage of £4 per week on 21 September 1951. This was about five shillings a week more than a clerk but with less chance of overtime pay.

I was just 21 and the youngest permanent stationmaster on British Railways. Much to my disgust, when my uniform arrived I found that a class 5 stationmaster did not warrant gold braid on his hat, only white piping which was almost indistinguishable from a guard.

Wyke & Norwood Green stood immediately at the end of Wyke tunnel. It was a timber structure with the booking office located on the central common overbridge with stairs leading to the up and down platforms. If a Bradford train stopped with its chimney directly underneath the booking office it would fill the place with choking sulphur fumes, soot, dirt and very hot air. We had to make a run for it every time the down train bell rang.

Staffing comprised, Stationmaster, two porters,

Laisterdyke Station was in a cutting at the summit of the Bradford to Leeds line. It had two island platforms. The cover over the near side staircase was blown off during an air raid about 1940.

(John Bateman)

early and late turn, and supervision of the signalbox at Wyke Junction. Staff shortage was chronic and the only porter, Jack Robershaw worked twelve hours a day, the remaining platform duties being covered by one of the signalmen on overtime. Porter's duties included weekly maintenance of the signal lamps. Because of the limited approach sighting on the up line coming out of the tunnel, the home signal was a tubular pole, extremely high and carrying signal arms both at the top and halfway up. In any sort of wind this pole swayed about alarmingly and took real courage to climb. Although we had an almost permanent request for porters at the local labour exchange, every applicant would bottle out when faced with this signal duty, leaving Jack to soldier on alone although well paid.

Freight traffic consisted almost entirely of wagonloads of ammonium picrate, a horrendous yellow powder which permeated anything with which it came into contact. The staff at A&H Marks & Co Ltd, responsible for unloading, were themselves as yellow coloured as the material. What Health and Safety would say today does not bear thinking about.

Passenger traffic was light so far as fare paying was concerned but heavy and constant with railway staff particularly drivers, firemen and shed staff to and from Low Moor and Bradford. The practice was that the fire in the down side porters room was never allowed to go out nor was the door ever locked. The room was used all day and all through the night by loco men taking shift duty. They would ring the signalbox, from the platform for a lift on the next down train or loco, which would stop and pick them up. Our bonus from this operation was that every loco which stopped would throw off a cwt of coal onto the platform to support the endless fire requirement. As a result on Monday mornings, Jack would often have to dig his way from the bottom of the steps to reach the platform and clear access for the passengers.

Regular stationmasters' meetings were held each month at Hunts Bank where the Divisional Superintendent, Mr Bannister would require each stationmaster publicly to explain and discuss any exceptional train delays on his section. Whilst we were advised in advance, it was still a formidable hurdle to stand up in front of one's peers for this purpose. I only attended one meeting at Manchester, arriving in my best suit which I had not worn since my wedding some six weeks earlier. On being called to "give evidence", I reached into my pocket for my notes and promptly showered everyone for three

rows in front with confetti, causing uproar and eventually being allowed to sit down.

On 21 September 1951, after only six weeks at Wyke, I was promoted to stationmaster (class 4) Northorpe North Road including Northorpe Higher again on the Cleckheaton branch and back in the Eastern Region under Wakefield District. Before I was allowed to take up this appointment, I was again required to undergo an oral examination in Block Rules & Regulations etc at Low Moor conducted by the area Signalling Inspector, the third such examination in six months. It sounds as if they didn't trust me.

Northorpe North Road Station was an imposing structure described by Thomas Normington as "More like a Bishops Palace than a station". Built in 1891 by the L&Y Railway, it was an island platform above the road level reached by a flight of stone steps from beneath the overbridge. It served the northern side of Ravensthorpe and originally would have provided a rail service for the workers at the many woollen mills and shoddy manufacturers located in the same area. Northorpe Higher station was some 500 yards further up the hill on the LNW line between Huddersfield and Leeds. Each station could clearly be seen from the other. Staffing at North Road was stationmaster and two leading porters. Lamping duties were included at Higher but not at North Road, as there were no signals in the section between Heckmondwike and Mirfield.

The station at Higher was a two platform timber construction with a principal booking office on the Down side and a secondary one on the Up line. Train services were infrequent over the Spen line and passenger revenue was light although evidence of busier times could be found in the large stock of tickets of all descriptions still maintained in the principal booking office drawers. One of my first tasks was to rationalise these stocks, reducing them to mainstream user. It took some considerable time organising approved withdrawal with the audit office. On call responsibility was vested in the stationmaster at Heckmondwike, George Smith during my off duty hours and at night.

The last stopping train at Northorpe Higher was in the Leeds direction. During 1952 the late turn porter/signalman was in the habit of catching this train to travel home. This required a quick run round, lock up, lights out and hop on the train routine. The down side office was heated by a cylindrical coke stove which could be filled and damped down overnight so the early turn staff had a warm office on arrival, simply needing to open up the dampers to get

Wyke & Norwood Green looking towards Bradford. This was a remote station at the entrance to Wyke Tunnel.

(B.C. Lane collection)

The island platform at Cleckheaton Central, looking towards Bradford. In 1970, a Mr. Reginald Sedgwick was found not guilty at Wakefield Crown Court of the theft of Cleckheaton Station. He had been accused of stealing large quantities of metal, stone and timber belonging to British Railways. The defendant pleaded successfully that he had acted in good faith on the instruction of a Mr. Watson who had promised him £400 to demolish the station but who had first relieved him of a £100 performance bond. Needless to say, Mr. Watson could no longer be found. *(Peter E. Baughan)*

the fire going. On this particular night however he failed to close down the stove. At about 01.30, the crew of a light engine observed the building glowing. On peering through the window, the driver saw a telephone and broke the glass to reach it. This allowed air to enter and explode the office into flames which rapidly spread to engulf the down side building. The timber platform was saved by the fire brigade. On my arrival next morning I was greeted by a smouldering ruin and hundreds upon hundreds of burnt and partly burnt ticket stocks blowing about the wreckage. Accountancy requirements meant that all such tickets should be accounted for but, to my relief, the Passenger Superintendent from Leeds, Mr Poulding, appeared during the morning and suggested that perhaps I could continue the fire and in so doing 'lose' the rest of the damaged ticket stock. The down side office was never rebuilt. A temporary hut was used until the station closed in October 1953. The leading porter/signalman responsible subsequently rose to become a senior signalman in Leeds City box.

During the years 1951-1954 I also was asked to "look on" at Battyeford Station incorporating Bradley which was then only used for Football specials for Huddersfield Town. The stationmaster post at Battyeford was a vacancy which because of its intended closure had not been advertised. Whilst passenger business was of a level similar to my own at Northorpe, the stationmaster Battyeford was responsible for the payment of wages for all staff of all departments between his station and Spen Valley Junction including several permanent way gangs and signal and telegraph staff. This necessitated a considerable walk along the track on Thursday mornings unsupervised.

I was also asked to "look on" at Ravensthorpe & Thornhill including Ravensthorpe Lower. Ravensthorpe & Thornhill was by LNW Junction alongside Thornhill Power Station on the Leeds to Huddersfield main line. Ravensthorpe Lower was un-staffed, situated on the branch from Heckmondwike to Thornhill. It was only used for occasional excursion trains, including one or two organised by the local working men's club.

During 1954 arrangements were set in motion to dispense with the Station Masters' posts at Battyeford and Northorpe North Road and extend the responsibility of the Heckmondwike Station Master giving George Smith a regrading to class 3. I was transferred to Ravensthorpe & Thornhill (class 4) on 4 October 1954 upon implementation of this arrangement.

As a footnote it is interesting that George Smith immediately applied for a class 2 post as stationmaster Morpeth, and was in fact appointed. Before he could take up the post, it was regraded to class 1 following an application by the previous incumbent which had been in the pipeline prior to the vacancy being advertised. The District Manager at Wakefield was incensed about this as George had rocketed from class 4 to 1 in the space of three months. He did his best to void the appointment without success. George moved and within a year was Special class A at Berwick upon Tweed. He had been in the right place at the right time.

I was myself assimilated into class 3 in 1955 when classes 4 and 3 were merged. It took me until 1960 to reach class 2 at Hemsworth.

A Week in the Life
of a frustrated traveller

For the past 38 years, my main involvement with the railway industry has been as a passenger. I have had a bit of operating experience in the preservation sector but otherwise I can write as no more than an 'informed traveller'.

Since 1981, my most frequent journey has been at one end of the Calder Valley route between New Pudsey and Halifax. As we glide past the queue of cars near Hipperholme it is almost time to put reading matter away. Once through Beacon Hill Tunnel, we'll be in Halifax Station and those car drivers will still be frustrated a few yards on from where we last saw them.

That's the feeling when things are going well but the railway is such an inflexible tool that the slightest problem, sometimes many miles away, can cause real difficulties. When I started writing the following piece on Thursday 6 May, I believed I was describing a typical week. The events of Saturday were more extreme but by no means unique.

If these notes should fall into the hands of railway managers, there is one major point which cannot be over-emphasised:

As often as not, delays to trains are only part of the problem. The effect on customers is compounded by lack of information and failure to use existing communication systems.

The Railway can be a very effective means of travel. Yet a majority of the mobile population would not think of journeying by anything other than car. The following paragraphs will do little to persuade them otherwise.

Monday 3 May 1999
Bank holiday but I have to visit the office. I travel New Pudsey to Halifax and back – no problems. I arrive New Pudsey at 15.50 in the hope of meeting Philippa who should be coming on the 16.01 in the other direction. She is returning from Rowlands Castle in Hampshire with luggage, one year old Adrian and push chair.

The 16.01 trains comes but no Philippa. Likewise the 16.14. The tannoy announces that the 16.28 is running 15 minutes late. It duly deposits Philippa at about 16.44. It is 16 minutes late, she 43 minutes.

Delay due to main line train held up at Retford (reason unknown) + 16.18 Leeds–Blackpool blocked in at Leeds for 15 minutes by driverless 16.08 Leeds–Liverpool. As a bonus, Philippa's train is overcrowded because it has also picked up customers for the subsequent train.

Tuesday 4 May
Destination Harrogate. My colleague, Glynis, needs to catch the 7.41 from Halifax connecting into the 8.29 from Leeds. I will not join her at New Pudsey but take a bus to Horsforth and board the train there.

The 7.41 from Halifax is cancelled, Glynis struggles to gain even a standing space on the 8.03. She gets a seat from Bradford but notices people being left behind at New Pudsey and Bramley. She reaches Harrogate 30 minutes late but only 20 minutes behind me. The 8.42 from Horsforth was itself 10 minutes late. No tannoy announcement was made at this unstaffed station to tell us when or if it was coming.

Return journey no problem.

Wednesday 5 May
I had persuaded Glynis that her only hope was to get the 7.25 from Halifax. Actually she caught the 7.17 running late. A trouble free journey to and from Harrogate today.

Thursday 6 May
Harrogate again. Glynis catches the 7.25 and comments favourably on the refurbished class 158. No problems today for her but at lunchtime I adjourn to a different client on the Hornbeam Park side of Harrogate. I don't finish work until about 18.35. The client drives me to Hornbeam Park Station for the 18.47. I have telephoned to ask Philippa (and Adrian) to pick me up in the car at Horsforth.

18.47 – no train – no tannoy announcement. By 19.00 I doubt if it is coming at all. Will Philippa be waiting at Horsforth similarly in the dark? Is it just this train which has blobbed or is there a blockage affecting the 19.17 as well? In other words, am I stranded here?

Question answered – the train appears. I ask the conductor what has happened? He professes not to understand the question. I explain that the train is 15 minutes late. I have been waiting on an unstaffed station with no public address announcements and my wife is probably in a similar position at Horsforth. He is polite and cheerful but can only offer me a complaint form – which I decline.

Philippa and Adrian are waiting at Horsforth. The public address there had remained silent until ten minutes after the train should have appeared. Only then was it announced as "running six minutes late". At least Philippa then had an idea that it was on its way.

Friday 7 May
Back to the more usual New Pudsey to Halifax routine. I experience no problems but Philippa, returning by the 17.42 from Halifax, is told to get off at Bradford, because the train is being terminated, and await the next one, 21 minutes later. No explanation given.

Saturday 8 May
This afternoon's mission is to get Adrian out in his push chair, give his mother a break and deliver some books to Ilkley. I walk to New Pudsey for the 14.01 with Adrian, his emergency rations, push chair and heavy shoulder bag containing the books.

14.01 – no train – no public address (the station is staffed mornings only but the tannoy is supposed to announce delays of five minutes or more)

14.14 – likewise.

I've clearly now missed the 14.27 from Bradford Forster Square to Ilkley. If the 14.28 from New Pudsey doesn't turn up, I'm going to abandon the trip altogether.

Unfortunately, in the light of subsequent events, a train does appear at 14.25. It takes us to Bradford Interchange. Here there are notices outlining the problem. Due to a serious signalling and points failure at Leeds, the service has been considerably thinned out. Alternate trains only are running through New Pudsey but Bradford to Ilkley is operating half hourly as normal. Off we trudge to Forster Square for the 14.57 to Ilkley.

At Bradford's other station we find no trains, the television screens all blank and the ticket office closed. Wait a moment. I am doing the ticket lady an injustice as she is out on the platform explaining to would be passengers that, although the Ilkley and Skipton trains were running normally this morning, they have been virtually stopped for the past hour and a half so she suggests that short distance passengers should go by bus. I've heard this story before and then a train has turned up. We wait for a few minutes before setting off back to Interchange Station. Our sole objective is now to get back home. I know the 15.18 to New Pudsey is cancelled but there is supposed to be one at

15.34 so there's no rush.

Why not call into Thomas Cook's for an up to date ferry timetable for a forthcoming trip to Ireland? They haven't got the leaflet required but the lady says she can get the information by telephone. I give it a go and she soon obtains a fare from New Pudsey through to Sligo. Can we break our journey in Dublin? She thinks not. Can we actually get through to Sligo the same day? She doesn't know. Apparently neither Thomas Cook or Stena Line have an Irish timetable and mine is at home. I ask if she has a Thomas Cook European Timetable. She says not but then remembers that they actually sell them so she borrows one.

At this point she advises me that, if I wish to make a booking, there will be a £10 per person booking fee on top of the fare. I respond that travel agents get a commission from the railway/shipping company. She says this isn't enough so they levy a surcharge with the result that many clients prefer to get the information from us but make the booking elsewhere. I express no surprise and wheel Adrian towards the station.

The lady in front of me asks the ticket man for the time of the next train to Leeds. He consults a computer and replies that the 15.34 is cancelled. She seems to accept this as a full answer and goes away. I am less easily fobbed off and, as a reward for my persistence, am invited to remove myself from the vicinity of the ticket office. This I do wheeling Adrian straight into the station supervisors office where I seek an apology and news of a train home.

They may be under pressure and are not personally responsible for the signal failure in Leeds but I have had a wasted afternoon, unable to reach my destination at Ilkley. As I do not have four arms, I cannot get Adrian, his pushchair, his tackle and the undelivered books onto a bus. I receive a coffee, the offer of baby changing facilities and an explanation that the signalling in Leeds has now failed completely. They promise to keep me informed.

I take the opportunity to pursue my enquiry about fares to Ireland and obtain comprehensive information as to which sailings are 'peak' and which 'off peak'. I am offered free reservations and no surcharge. I don't book now in case a train comes in the middle of the transaction.

Eventually we get home on a slightly late running 16.34.

Sunday 9 May

No rail travel today. It's not for lack of Sunday trains. They generally run at half the weekday frequency. Today I must get those books to Ilkley. No messing, they're going by car.

But not until we get a new exhaust fitted. It's suddenly blown and the car sounds like a motorbike.

Is any transport trouble free?

Post Script

The following week was much better. No serious problems. There was even a tannoy announcement at Headingley when a train was running just three minutes late. And I booked the tickets to Ireland at New Pudsey station.

My ultimate destination. From the early 1920s until we moved in 1999, Sutcliffe & Riley, Chartered Accountants were based in the upper floor of Fountain Chambers, Halifax. In 1935, I could have travelled up from the station on an electric tram or maybe hitched a lift on the LMS mechanical horse at the bottom right.
(Sutcliffe & Riley collection)

Class Distinction

By offering three classes of accommodation, the early railways merely reflected contemporary society. The different carriages were broadly aimed at the upper, middle and lower classes. These groups could afford differential fares and probably didn't want to mix on the journey with people outside of their own station.

Most importantly, the three classes offered roughly equal sizes of market. Notwithstanding that the middle class were far more numerous than their 'betters', their travel habit was less developed. And as for the workers, they were by far the most numerous but their need to travel was almost non-existent.

Some railway companies thought they were providing a social service by offering third class travel at all. They felt no commercial or other pressure to worry about the standard of accommodation and service.

Gradually, during the Victorian period, the lot of the third class passenger improved under a combination of legislation and commercial reality. The railway companies could not ignore an increasingly mobile 90% of the population. As third class became available on all trains and as the standard of accommodation improved, the companies discovered the scale of waste involved in dragging around three classes of carriage especially for local journeys where typically 97% of travel was third class with the balance divided between first and second. The result was abolition of the second class.

The Lancashire & Yorkshire Railway did not take the lead in this process but was compelled to respond, eventually, to developments on neighbouring lines. The Midland Railway carried third class passengers on all trains from 1872 and abolished second class in 1875. The corresponding dates for the Lancashire & Yorkshire were 1878 and 1912.

For legal reasons, the designation third class had to be retained. It was not until 1956 that it was renamed second on a Europe wide basis. Some countries, including our own, now call it 'standard'.

That still left most local trains conveying a usually empty first class coach or part coach. In an age when passenger trains could also afford plenty of van space, they didn't seem too bothered. Only on lines worked by rail motors or short fixed formations did they advertise 'third class only'.

When British Railways introduced its diesel multiple unit fleet between 1954 and 1961, two classes were still the norm. The class 110 Calder Valley sets had a total of 24 first class seats situated in the two end most compartments. At least this position meant that nobody except the driver had any reason to pass through the first class sections. It also gave passengers a coveted view of the line ahead which will have led to the occasional sale of first class tickets to connoisseurs seeking this privilege.

It is my recollection that the facility was not widely abused even though the checking of tickets on trains was virtually unknown in those days. It was generally seen as forbidden territory through which you had no reason to pass. And there was a vestibule door which took some muscle to open.

If the second class was overcrowded, then passengers would gingerly venture into the first class usually with nobody to question them. The absence of second class seats worked as a good excuse in practice, even though it had no legal standing.

A fellow Chartered Accountant once told me that the way to commute first class cheaply was to buy a

You get a table lamp, a power socket and a head rest cover.   *(Martin Bairstow)*

first class ordinary return (valid for three months) and keep it in one's wallet either until challenged or until the expiry of three months. Meanwhile buy a second class day return for each trip. I'm sure he was only testing the system, not abusing it.

By the 1980's, the diesel trains were decidedly shabby and it was increasingly rare for anybody to pay first class on routes such as Calder Valley. The PTEs took both a practical and political objection to the continuing practice which was abolished in January 1983.

The second generation dmus, introduced from 1987, joined a one class establishment. With most trains formed of only two coaches, with no van space and with traffic rising, there was simply no room for an empty first class section.

But the privatised owners of Northern Spirit thought otherwise and gave a franchise commitment to reintroduce first class on 'Trans Pennine' trains. Refurbished class 158s began to appear in 1999 with 16 first class seats per two car set and 32 on a three car. At first, the 'Trans Pennine Express' to Blackpool enjoyed an exemption – the first class designation was ignored until 17 January 2000 when it began to be enforced. In practice, half the Blackpool trains are formed of rolling stock which remains standard class only.

The first class fare is by means of a supplement payable on the train which, on average, doubles the price. It doesn't apply if trains with a first class section turn up on local journeys including those to Manchester Victoria.

As an almost daily user of the Calder Valley Line, I can find nothing to support the move back to first class. Given how busy many of the trains are, the system would work only if the customers divided themselves more or less in direct proportion to the number of first and standard class seats. This would require something between a coincidence and a miracle. The practice is that the trains carry a minimal number of people actually paying the supplement – as opposed to gate crashers and holders of current and retired staff passes.

On the busiest trains they now crowd people into the remaining $1\frac{3}{4}$ or $2\frac{1}{2}$ coaches. As they stand, squat or sit on the luggage shelves, passengers have the additional irritation of seeing the largely empty first class section. Alternatively they abandon the distinction for the duration of the overcrowding or it abandons itself through sheer weight of numbers. This means that anyone who has paid the supplement suffers the same overcrowding as the rest of us.

Conclusion

Railways were born of the Industrial Revolution. They thrived on heavy staple industry especially coal. At a time when transport by other means was very difficult, the railways carried all manner of traffic.

It is fascinating to see how they went about their business using methods which were once at the forefront of technology. Many features continued well into our lifetimes so this book has been able to portray both images and first hand experiences from the steam age.

It is one thing to reminisce about Victorian operating methods and equipment. It is a very different matter trying to perpetuate them into an era of motorways and mass car ownership. Yet this is largely what British Railways tried to do – or at least failed to avoid doing. The transition to a modern railway has been a painful process with many mistakes along the way.

Today's railway is largely a high density passenger operation. It is a growth industry thanks to ever increasing car ownership. How ironic this statement may sound. But cars no longer threaten rail traffic, they encourage it both by creating congestion and by affording easier access to the rail network.

On the freight side, the battle has largely been lost. For passengers, most services are better than ever before. The greatest problem now, touched upon in the last few pages, is poor reliability, sometimes aggravated by overcrowding. Unless of course, you want to go to Cleckheaton, Lightcliffe or Elland ...

Appendices

The Calder Valley Line

Opened

4. 7.1839	Manchester Oldham Road - Littleborough
5.10.1840	Normanton-Hebden Bridge
31.12.1840	Hebden Bridge-Summit Tunnel (East)
1. 3.1841	Summit Tunnel (East)-Littleborough
1. 1.1844	Manchester Victoria-Miles Platting
1. 7.1844	Greetland-Halifax
9. 5.1850	Low Moor-Bradford Exchange
9. 5.1850	Halifax-Low Moor
–	
1. 1.1852	Sowerby Bridge-Halifax
1. 8.1854	Bowling Junction-Leeds Central
1. 8.1854	Bradford Adolphus St-Laisterdyke
29.10.1877	Manchester Loop Line (goods)
1. 8.1878	Manchester Loop Line (passenger)

Closed to passenger traffic

31.12.1843	Manchester Oldham Road-Miles Platting
31.12.1961	Bowling Junction-Laisterdyke
29. 4.1967	Holbeck-Leeds Central
4. 1.1970	Halifax/Sowerby Bridge-Mirfield

Closed to all traffic

29. 4.1967	Holbeck-Leeds Central
1982	Manchester Oldham Road-Miles Platting
1985	Bowling Junction-Laisterdyke
12. 9.1998	Manchester Loop Line

Stations reopened

12. 9.1983	Bramley
29. 3.1985	Mills Hill
19. 8.1985	Smithy Bridge
10. 9.1990	Walsden
28. 5.2000	Brighouse

Miles	Stations	Opened	Closed
0	Manchester Victoria	1.1.1844	–
–	Manchester Oldham Road	4.7.1839	31.12.1843
1½	Miles Platting	1.1.1844	–
2¾	Newton Heath	1.12.1853	1.1.1966
4	Moston	Feb 1872	–
5¼	Middleton Junction	31.3.1842	1.1.1966
5¼	Mills Hill	4.7.1839	11.8.1842
9	Castleton (Blue Pits)	4.7.1839	
10½	Rochdale	4.7.1839	–
12¾	Smithy Bridge	Oct. 1868	1.5.1960
13¾	Littleborough	4.7.1839	–
17¾	Ealsden	Nov 1845	6.8.1961
19¼	Todmorden	31.12.1840	1.12.1951
21½	Eastwood	31.12.1840	1.12.1951
23½	Hedben Bridge	5.10.1840	–
24¾	Mytholmroyd	May 1847	–
26½	Luddendenfoot	5.10.1840	8.9.1962
28½	Sowerby Bridge	5.10.1840	–
31	Greetland (North Dean)	1.7.1884	8.9.1962
3¼	Elland	Mar 1841	8.9.1962
34¼	Brighouse	5.10.1840	31.1.1970
36½	Cooper Bridge	5.10.1840	31.12.1960
38½	Mirfield	Apr 1845	–
40¾	Thornhill (Dewsbury)	5.10.1840	31.12.1961
44	Horbury & Ossett	5.10.1840	3.1.1970
45	Horbury Millfield Road	11.7.1927	4.11.1961
45½	Horbury Junction	1.1.1850	31.12.1961
47¾	Wakefield Kirkgate	5.10.1840	18.2.1950
50¾	Normanton	1.7.1840	–
61	Leeds Hunslet Lane	1.7.1840	–
30¾	Copley	Nov 1855	18.7.1931
32¼	Halifax	1.7.1844	
34¼	Hipperholme	7.8.1850	6.6.1953
35	Lightcliffe	7.8.1850	12.6.1965
36¼	Wyke & Norwood Green	7.8.1850	19.9.1953
38	Low Moor	18.7.1848	12.6.1965
39¾	Bowling Junction	1.2.1902	1.12.1951
41	Bradford Exchange	9.5.1850	–
–	Bradford Adolphus Street	1.8.1854	6.1.1867
40½	Bowling	1.8.1854	31.1.1895
41½	Laisterdyke	1.8.1854	2.7.1966
43	New Pudsey	6.3.1967	–
44	Stanningley	1.8.1854	30.12.1967
45¼	Bramley	1.8.1854	2.7.1966
47	Armley Moor	1.8.1854	2.7.1966
48½	Holbeck	2.7.1855	5.7.1958
49	Leeds Central	18.9.1848	29.4.1967
49	Leeds City	30.6.1846	-

The Oldham Branch

Opened

31. 3.1842	Middleton Junction-Oldham Werneth
1.11.1847	Oldham Werneth-Oldham Mumps
12. 8.1863	Oldham Mumps-Rochdale (goods)
2.11.1863	Oldham Mumps-Rochdale (passenger)
21. 3.1864	Royton Junction-Royton
17. 5.1880	Thorpes Bridge Jn-Oldham Werneth
12. 8.1914	Middleton Junction-Chadderton (goods)

Miles	Stations	Opened	Closed
0	Manchester Victoria	1.1.1844	–
1½	Miles Platting 1.1.1844	–	
2¾	Dean Lane	17.5.1880	–
3¾	Failsworth	Apr 1881	–
4¾	Hollinwood	17.5.1880	
6½	Oldham Werneth	31.3.1842	–
7	Oldham Central	Jul 1861	16.4.1966
7½	Oldham Mumps	1.11.1847	–

Closure to passenger traffic

9. 6.1958	Middleton Junction-Oldham Werneth	8¼		Derker	30.9.1985	–
16. 4.1966	Royton Junction-Royton	8½		Royton Junction	1.7.1864	9.5.1987
	Closure to all traffic	9¾		Royton	21.3.1864	16.4.1966
5. 1.1963	Middleton Junction-Oldham Werneth	10¼		Shaw & Crompton	2.11.1863	–
16. 4.1966	Royton Junction-Royton	12		New Hey	2.11.1863	
1987	Middleton Junction-Chadderton	13		Milnrow	2.11.1863	
		14¾		Rochdale	4.7.1839	–

The Middleton Branch

	Opened 5.1.1857	0		Middleton Junction	31.3.1842	1.1.1966
	Closed 5.9.1964 (passenger)	1		Middleton	5.1.1857	5.9.1964
	9.10.1965 (goods)					

The Bacup Branch

	Opened	0		Rochdale	4.7.1839	–
5.10.1870	Rochdale-Facit (goods)	1¼		Wardleworth	1.11.1870	14.6.1947
1.11.1870	Rochdale-Facit (passenger)	3		Shawclough & Healey	1.11.1870	14.6.1947
1.12.1881	Facit-Bacup	3¾		Bradley	1.11.1870	14.6.1947
	Closed to passengers 14.6.1947	4¾		Whitworth	1.11.1870	14.6.1947
	Closed to all traffic	5¾		Facit	1.11.1870	14.6.1947
10.10.1954	Facit-Bacup	6¾		Shawforth	1.12.1881	14.6.1947
10.87.1963	Whitworth-Facit	7½		Britannia	1.12.1881	2.4.1917
19. 8.1967	Rochdale-Whitworth	9		Bacup	1.10.1852	3.12.1966

The Copy Pit Route

	Opened	0		Todmorden	31.12.1840	–
12.11.1849	Todmorden-Burnley	½		Stansfield Hall	Aug 1869	29.7.1944
Sept 1850	Burnley-Gannow Junction	2		Cornholme	Jul 1878	24.9.1938
Mar 1862	Hall Royd Junction-Stansfield Hall	3¼		Portsmouth	12.11.1849	5.7.1958
	Closed	5½		Holme	12.11.1849	27.7.1930
8.11.1965	Todmorden-Stansfield Hall (passenger)	8¼		Towneley	12.11.1849	2.8.1952
Mar 1973	Todmorden-Stansfield Hall (goods)	8¾		Burnley Manchester Road	12.11.1849	5.11.1961
	Burnley Manchester Road reopened 13.10.1986	9¾		Rose Grove	18.9.1848	

The Rishworth Branch

	Opened	0		Sowerby Bridge	5.10.1840	–
1. 7.1878	Sowerby Bridge-Ripponden (goods)	¾		Watsons Crossing	1.3.1907	6.7.1929
5. 8.1878	Sowerby Bridge-Ripponden (passenger)	1½		Triangle	1.6.1885	6.7.1929
1. 3.1881	Ripponden-Rishworth	3¼		Ripponden & Barkisland	5.8.1878	6.7.1929
	Closed	3¾		Risworth	1.8.1881	6.7.1929
6. 7.1929	Sowerby Bridge-Rishworth (passenger)					
10. 2.1953	Ripponden-Rishworth (all traffic)					
30. 8.1958	Sowerby Bridge-Ripponden (all traffic)					

The Stainland Branch

	Opened 1.1.1875	0		Greetland	1.7.1844	8.9.1962
	Closed 21.9.1929 (passenger)	¼		Rochdale Road	1.3.1907	21.9.1929
	Closed 12.9.1959 (all traffic)	½		West Vale	1.1.1875	21.9.1929
		1¼		Stainland & Holywell Green	1.1.1875	21.9.1929

The Spen Valley and Dewsbury Branches

	Opened	0		Low Moor	18.7.1848	12.6.1965
18. 7.1848	Low Moor-Mirfield	2½		Cleckheaton Central	18.7.1848	12.6.1965
10. 5.1869	Heckmondwike-Thornhill (goods)	3¾		Liversedge Central	18.7.1848	12.6.1965
30. 6.1869	Heckmondwike-Thornhill (passenger)	4¾		Heckmondwike Central	18.7.1848	12.6.1965
1. 4.1867	Thornhill-Dewsbury Market Place	6¼		Northorpe North Road	1.12.1891	12.6.1965
	Closed to passengers	7¾		Mirfield	Apr 1845	–
30.12.1961	Heckmondwike-Thornhill	6½		Ravensthorpe	Jul 1869	28.6.1952
12. 6.1965	Low Moor-Thornhill	7¼		Thornhill	5.10.1840	31.12.1961
	Closed to all traffic	9		Dewsbury Market Place	1.4.1867	30.11.1930
12. 6.1965	Heckmondwike-Mirfield					
1981	Low Moor-Heckmondwike					

The Pickle Bridge Branch

	Opened 1.3.1881	0		Wyke & Norwood Green	7.8.1850	19.9.1953
	Closed June 1948 (passengers)	1¼		Bailiff Bridge	1.3.1881	2.4.1917
	2.8.1952 (all traffic)	2¾		Clifton Road, Brighouse	1.3.1881	12.9.1931

Acknowledgements

I would like to thank the many people who have helped with this publication. The photographs are credited individually. The excursion leaflets are from the collections of David Beeken and David R Smith, the tickets from Geoffrey Lewthwaite. The signal diagrams were drawn by Richard Pulleyn from information supplied by Tony Ross. The manuscript was typed by Glynis and Jayne at Sutcliffe & Riley, Chartered Accountants. Additional information was supplied by Stuart Baker and Stuart Carmichael, also by some of the photographers. Thanks to Les Hoyle for his article. I acknowledge delving into John Marshall's three volume history of the Lancashire & Yorkshire Railway, also various L & Y Society branch line booklets.